CW00427969

# ROMAN
## MILITARY
## SIGNALLING

# ROMAN
# MILITARY
# SIGNALLING

## D.J. WOOLLISCROFT

TEMPUS

First published 2001

PUBLISHED IN THE UNITED KINGDOM BY:

Tempus Publishing Ltd
The Mill, Brimscombe Port
Stroud, Gloucestershire GL5 2QG
www.tempus-publishing.com

PUBLISHED IN THE UNITED STATES OF AMERICA BY:

Tempus Publishing Inc.
2 Cumberland Street
Charleston, SC 29401
1-888-313-2665
www.arcadiapublishing.com

Tempus books are available in France and Germany
from the following addresses:

Tempus Publishing Group          Tempus Publishing Group
21 Avenue de la République       Gustav-Adolf-Straße 3
37300 Joué-lès-Tours             99084 Erfurt
FRANCE                           GERMANY

© D.J. Woolliscroft, 2001

The right of D.J. Woolliscroft to be identified as the Author
of this work has been asserted by him in accordance with the
Copyrights, Designs and Patents Act 1988.

All rights reserved. No part of this book may be reprinted or reproduced or utilised in any form
or by any electronic, mechanical or other means, now known or hereafter invented, including
photocopying and recording, or in any information storage or retrieval system, without the
permission in writing from the Publishers.

British Library Cataloguing in Publication Data.
A catalogue record for this book is available from the British Library.

ISBN 0 7524 1938 2

Typesetting and origination by Tempus Publishing.
PRINTED AND BOUND IN GREAT BRITAIN

# Contents

# List of illustrations

# Acknowledgements

The author would like to thank the following for their help and advice or for assistance in the research for this book and in the field: Prof. E. Birley, Prof. A.R. Birley, Prof. A.S. Robinson, Prof. J.K. St Joseph, Prof. D. Baatz, Prof. L.J.F. Keppie, Prof. D.J. Breeze, Dr G. Simpson, Dr V.A. Maxfield, Mr G.S. Maxwell, Dr P.A. Holder, Dr C.S. Sommer, Dr N.J. Lockett, Dr A.G. Keen, Mr R.E. Birley and the staff of the Vindolanda Trust, Mr G. Bailey, Mr I. Caruana, Major G.H. Donaldson, Mr F. Kitchen, Mr P. Topping, Mrs K. Brown, Dr J. Pickin, Mr J. Walker, Dr and Mrs M.D. Nevell, Miss S. Baker, Mr M.T. Murphy, Mrs A. Bailey, Mr G. Jackson, Mr C. Hartley, Miss S. Sant, Herr B. Steidl, Miss E.A. Owens, Mr J. Macdonald, Mr B. Waslyn, Mr D. Pierce, Mr M. Mortimore and especially to Prof. G.D.B. Jones, Dr J.P. Wild, Dr B. Dobson, Frau G. Zorn, Dr S.A.M. Swain, Dr B. Hoffmann, Mr R.L. Bellhouse and my parents Mr and Mrs J. and V.F. Woolliscroft. I would also thank the libraries of the University of Durham, Keel, Newcastle-Upon-Tyne and Freiburg as well as the DAAD for funding my German work, and the Landesdenkmalämter for Baden-Württemberg and Hessen for their kind assistance and for access to material.

My thanks go also to the shades of those of the departed without whom my work would have been impossible.

# Introduction

This book is a study of the technology and capabilities of ancient military signalling, but it is also an attempt to investigate an important aspect of Roman frontier design. Defence systems of the huge size and complexity of Rome's fortified land frontiers, like all systems, required co-ordination and this meant that communications networks were needed to link them together. This much might go without saying, but the sheer scale of the systems means that the problems involved are hard to exaggerate. For these frontiers can be hundreds of miles long and often involve many hundreds of separate installations (ranging from watchtowers to legionary fortresses), all of which needed to be welded into a single integrated whole. Moreover, it was not enough that this might be achieved as an occasional drill exercise; it was essential that it could be maintained as a matter of reliable routine, from minute to minute, 24 hours a day and in all weathers, over timescales that can often be measured in centuries. For the most part, the vast bulk of such communications would probably have been by messenger, but the distances involved in even local communications on these lines can be considerable and, in a crisis, at least basic information would have needed more rapid transmission. This would have required some form of signalling system but, despite much speculation, the workings of such systems have rarely been convincingly explained. It is of some importance that Roman frontier signalling arrangements be investigated, or where appropriate shown to exist, for without them the Roman military would have rapidly lost co-ordination. It is not enough, however, simply to understand their workings. We also need to gauge their likely effectiveness and to see what, if any, influence the needs of signalling had on the overall design and layout of Roman frontier works. This should allow us to judge what importance the Romans placed upon them, which may, in turn, give us an indirect measure of the amount of signal traffic, in other words the amount of trouble, that was expected by the systems' designers. We may also gain a rare insight into the inner mechanisms of Roman frontiers, which may help us to understand the still debated issues of why such systems were built, how they were designed to work and what they were intended to achieve.

The book is divided into two main sections. Part 1 will review the technology of signalling in Roman times, in concert with a collection of ancient source material which has been gathered in Appendix 1. Part 2 will consist of a series of in-depth case studies of the design and signalling systems of two specific Roman frontiers: Hadrian's Wall, in Britain, and the *Limes* in southern Germany. Both appear to demonstrate that Roman frontiers were capable of operating highly effective signalling systems and that these exercised a considerable influence on the frontiers' overall design. Hopefully they will be informative in their own right, as well as addressing the questions outlined above. But they also suggest that a study of the signalling system of any Roman frontier might help us to gain a greater understanding of the spatial and chronological relationships between known sites on or near the frontier and even to discover new ones.

There is too a wider question to be addressed. One of the most striking features of the early imperial Roman army, throughout the Empire, is the high, if sometimes exaggerated, level of uniformity of its equipment and organisation. In particular, we have grown used to the idea that the design of Roman forts and other military installations will be much the same, wherever they are found. It is, therefore, interesting to consider the possibility that the scale of such conformity may have extended still further to encompass the second-century Empire's vast and elaborate frontiers. Certainly, given the high degree of standardisation of other aspects of Roman military construction, a broad uniformity of frontier design should come as little surprise, especially since most such systems, however different they may look on the ground, break down into the same three basic elements (but see Mann 1974). Details may differ, as do the often lengthy evolutionary processes by which any one frontier reached its ultimate form, but the classic Roman *Limes* almost always rests on a combination of a frontier line (with or without a running barrier), an observation screen, based on a system of watchtowers, and a series of principal garrison forts backed by, sometimes distant, legionary bases (Jones, G.D.B. 1978).

There are, of course, very real differences between individual frontiers and these are both fascinating and of obvious importance. Yet, whilst modern studies rightly continue to reveal and emphasise them, we should not allow an immense and growing wealth of archaeological minutiae to blind us to any signs of an underlying uniformity. Ultimately, therefore, the question to be asked is simple. Was each Roman frontier a totally unique design with its own set of operating procedures, in the same way that each had its own physical peculiarities of construction and fortification? Or can we instead begin to speak of some sort of unified, Empire-wide, frontier blueprint or principle, however diffuse, under which all Rome's linear frontiers operated in the same basic fashion? If the first option is true, then standardisation breaks down at this level. But the second would mean that the apparently considerable differences between frontiers may, in reality, be only relatively superficial peculiarities dictated by local factors such as terrain, operational conditions and the availability of materials, time and manpower.

Possible intermediate positions must also be borne in mind. For example, at the time the first frontier systems were being built, in the AD 80s (Woolliscroft forthcoming b), the once fluid and highly mobile provincial armies were beginning the slow process that was eventually to fossilise them into more or less distinct and permanent regional groupings, each of which may have developed its own solutions to frontier design. This would mean that similarities between different frontiers in the same province may only show that that particular army was consistent in following its own way of doing things and need not necessarily shed light on other provinces, which may have been operating quite differently. This, in turn, means that no study of Roman frontier design can afford to confine itself to a single province or even, perhaps, to a single tight regional grouping of provinces; hence the choice of the *Limes* in the provinces of Germania Superior and Raetia as a comparison to Roman Britain.

The present work can probably not expect to give final, or definitive, answers to these questions, but it will provide a great deal of new data as well as offering a slightly different way of looking at the problems. It is also hoped that it will, at least, allow us to begin to look more closely into the possibility of a universal frontier design and to try to isolate which, if any, aspects of a particular system's layout may be part of this plan and which are adaptations to local circumstances.

## Methodology

There has been only one other book on ancient signalling: Wolfgang Leiner's *Der Signaltechnik Der Antike*, published in 1982. This well-researched work has proved very useful and deserves to be better known, but it was limited by the fact that it dealt exclusively with information contained in ancient written accounts. This source material is, of course, vital, but the present book attempts to go a step further by evaluating performance data obtained through experiments with reconstructed signalling equipment. This was then applied to real Roman frontier works on the ground and it is worth outlining the field methodology used.

In the absence of modern electronic communications, Roman signalling relied on visual methods, except over very short ranges. It is, therefore, vital for any understanding of the signalling system of a Roman frontier to study the fields of view of the installations that make it up, and especially their ability to see (and thus signal to) one another. In theory, this can be done using large-scale contour maps, but, for two reasons, it was thought best that the site intervisibilities should always be checked in the field. Firstly, even 1:10,000 scale maps with close contour intervals are not accurate enough to show conclusively whether or not many borderline sites could see each other. Secondly, it was felt that if signalling had influenced a frontier's design, subtle variations in its layout, and their relationship to the terrain, would be far easier to detect and explain on the ground. The results gained through this policy have amply justified the considerable extra work involved, especially as they now rest on data whose reliability can be guaranteed.

On each of the frontiers studied, the programme of work was simply to visit every Roman installation on the system (or a substantial sample thereof) and compile a list of every other Roman site each could see, along with a note of any relevant topographical points. The intervisibility patterns thus obtained were then studied to determine what, if any, signalling system could have been in operation and whether the overall design of the frontier had been adapted to accommodate it. Two problems had been anticipated, however, and techniques were devised to overcome them. The most important was the question of the height from which the ancient signallers would have worked. For the Romans were not restricted to operating from the surface; they could also employ the better viewpoints provided by a variety of fort, fortlet and independent frontier towers. Today, many of these installations are obscured from one another, at ground level, by the terrain and it was important to test whether or not such sites would have been intervisible from their full tower height. To this end a method of low-level aerial photography was contrived (Woolliscroft 1989b) in which a camera was mounted on the end of a telescopic pole which, when held above the head, allowed photographs to be taken from an altitude of approximately 7m using the self timer (**1**). This is probably slightly lower than the full height of a Roman watchtower. But, in most cases, it proved sufficient, and equipment strong enough to carry a camera to a more realistic *c*.10m would have been less portable and more difficult to operate.

Neither ground observation nor elevated photography could penetrate even light modern tree cover, however. Where this was present, a version of the Romans' own visual signalling was used in which a powerful electronic flash gun was fired at night from the top of the camera staff on one site, towards an observer on a target site. The observer was then able to report back whether or not the flash was visible using Citizen Band radio, giving this technique the secondary advantage that the results were known instantly rather than after film processing. The use of radio also allowed the repetition of doubtful tests and the testing of a number of sites in one run. Where necessary, the occasional use of a more lightweight flash attached to the main camera staff by means of a long dowel also allowed sites to be tested from the likely full *c*.10m tower height. Alternatively, when even this was not enough, the tower of the target site could be mimicked, on dark nights, by raising a camera on a second staff with its shutter locked open, so that the film would register a spark, or loom, of light if the flash was visible and nothing if it was not. Indeed, flash testing proved itself to be such a quick, flexible, yet definitive way of testing doubtful lines of sight that it is tempting to wonder whether the Romans may have used some similar technique, perhaps using elevated torches, in establishing those lines in the first place. Areas of really dense modern forest defeated all direct visual testing techniques and were avoided, where possible, in the initial choice of study area. Otherwise, their intervisibilities were worked out by map and, where necessary, rechecked by ground surveys which, occasionally, involved the re-levelling of parts of a line of sight.

## The choice of research targets

Hadrian's Wall and the German Limes were chosen for study for a number of different reasons. Firstly, as already stated, it seemed important to look at frontiers that were far enough apart and built by sufficiently separate army groupings that they were not likely to represent manifestations of the same purely regional design tradition. Secondly, no meaningful study of a frontier's signalling arrangements can be made unless the bulk of that system's component sites are already known and reasonably closely dated. This means that a signalling survey can only take place on a frontier whose basic anatomy has already been intensively investigated, either in whole, or at least over substantial stretches. Where this groundwork is lacking there may be too many gaps in the system for its signalling pattern to emerge, and there is too great a risk of projecting links between non-contemporary sites. Sadly, all too few Roman frontiers have yet been studied in sufficient detail and, for the moment at least, large areas of the Eastern and North African frontiers, as well as parts of the Rhine and Danube riverine systems, are still too poorly understood for this purpose. In particular, none of the wholly late frontiers, such as the Saxon Shore and Yorkshire Coast defences in Britain, are yet

*1 The author's elevated camera tower*

sufficiently well understood to allow a signalling survey, which has, unfortunately, prevented me from looking at how such systems evolved in the late Empire. Finally, given the insistence on personally collected field data, cost became a major consideration and the two frontiers chosen were simply the most economical systems to work on which also fulfilled the criteria outlined above.

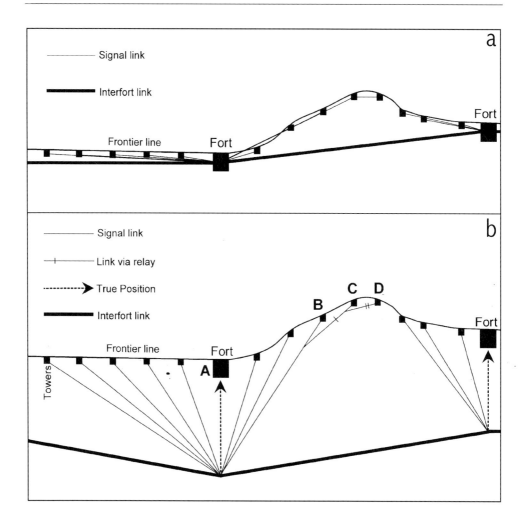

*2   Alternative means of representing frontier signalling systems*

## Illustrating signalling networks diagrammatically

It has proved surprisingly difficult to portray frontier signalling networks graphically in a way which still preserves geographical information; in other words, in a way which overlays a representation of the network onto a straightforward map of the frontier. Most of the signals traffic on a Roman frontier seems likely to have been alert warnings between the watchtowers spread out along the line itself and their parent forts, and the most obvious approach is simply to draw lines to represent the links involved. Unfortunately, as is shown by **2a**, these lines often run on top of one another and may pass through more than one line installation, which makes it hard to show the full system clearly or to differentiate between a direct link and a link via a relay. In short, such diagrams confuse as much as they inform. Worse still, the forts themselves could often be linked together (indeed some frontier forts are actually intervisible) and, although the easiest way to differentiate these links has been to use heavier lines, these have a tendency to block out the others and further obscure the pattern. To clarify matters, a compromise has been adopted in which a schematic signals network is superimposed onto a map of the frontier itself.

The results may need a little explanation, however. When, as is common on some frontiers, the forts are set back from the line, it is still possible to show the strict reality as the signal lines from the towers then remain separate on the drawings. Where the forts are built on the frontier itself, as on **2b**, however, the lines have been shown diagrammatically as though the forts were set back. In other words an arbitrary spot behind each fort's true position has been picked and the signal lines run to it. This random spot is then linked to the fort with a dotted, arrowed line to show that this is the signals' true destination. In **2b**, therefore, all of the towers between the left-hand side of the picture and the site marked B are intervisible with the fort marked A and can thus signal to it directly. Any sites whose signals would have needed relaying before they could reach a fort are then shown by means of a line with a cross, running into the relaying site's own signal line to the fort. One of these cross lines is used for each relay needed so, for example, on **2b**, tower C (with one cross) needs just one relay via tower B before its signals can reach fort A, whilst tower D (with two crosses) needs two relays via towers B and C.

# 1  Ancient signalling techniques

For as long as men have held power over others, the powerful have needed to gain information from beyond their field of vision and to send instructions beyond the range of their voices. References to the use of messengers and relay riders are thus commonplace in ancient literature, but wartime often required faster means of communication. Over short distances, on the battlefield itself, flags and standards were used to co-ordinate action, whilst at slightly longer ranges, in the words of one anonymous Byzantine writer (Anon. Byz. 262a), 'The trumpet might have been invented to allow generals to give orders to their troops.' Indeed sound-based signalling can operate over surprisingly long distances in the right conditions and we have one ancient account of relays of shouted messages being used to signal across mountainous parts of Persia (Appendix 1: 38). This may sound implausible, but it should be remembered that yodelling began as a means of communicating over similar terrain in the Alps. Nevertheless, the range of such methods remains limited and most long distance signalling in the ancient world seems to have relied on visual methods, many of which made use of fire.

Modern military communications often lie at the forefront of technology and there are signs that a great deal of care and ingenuity also went into the ancient techniques. Sadly, the aristocratic writers to whom we owe much of our knowledge of Roman history generally showed little interest in mechanical details and even more technically minded Greek writers are often little better. Nevertheless, a few sources do cast light on signals technology and a selection of the more informative have been collected in Appendix 1. A number of different methods, of varying sophistication, emerge from these sources and this chapter will look at each in turn to examine its workings, capabilities and limitations.

## Beacons and beacon chains

By far the most frequently mentioned signal transmitters in the ancient sources are simple fire beacons, and the 23 examples cited in Appendix 1 are only a sample of the many accounts that have come down to us. Their use seems to be very ancient, for they were mentioned by Homer (Appendix 1: 1) in (or around) the eighth century BC, and they continued in service into early modern times with, for example, the English Armada Beacons. Indeed a number of English settlements, such as the Cumbrian town of Penrith, maintained beacons up to the late eighteenth century (Kitchen 1988 and Ferguson 1897).

The beacon has a number of advantages as a signalling medium. It can combine to form chains and relay networks (Appendix 1: 2, 7 & 14). It produces both smoke, visible by day, and light, visible at night, and can thus be used 24 hours a day. It is fast and, as transmission involves no more than lighting a fire, it requires little in the way of equipment or expert personnel. This latter point is consistent with what little we know about the ancient signallers themselves, for although by the Byzantine Period they had acquired the Greek name of 'Semeiophoroi' (Appendix 1: 46), there seems to be no Latin word for signaller. This suggests that the role was not regarded as a specialised one in the Roman army and so required little in the way of professional training (Donaldson 1988, 351). The sources which deal with the issue (Appendix 1: 33 & 52) suggest that signallers should be drawn from the ordinary ranks and chosen, not for skill or dedicated training, but for trustworthiness, to avoid betrayal, for courage, to remain at sometimes dangerous posts, for sufficient war experience to be able to correctly interpret events, so as not to signal (or refrain from signalling) inappropriately, and for running speed, to bring messages quickly on foot should signalling fail. The sources do stress the importance of preparation but, although there is one reference to an army commander personally selecting a signalling position (Appendix 1: 26), they do not appear to have expected much skill to be involved in transmitting.

Beacons can also operate over surprisingly long ranges. U.S. Coast and Geodetic Survey experiments at the end of the nineteenth century (Merriam 1890, p26ff) showed that, when used on a clear night between mountain tops, a large beacon fire can be seen from as far away as 160-200 miles. There are no ancient references to signalling over quite these immense distances, but beacon signals could certainly cross many tens of miles. The most interesting, if controversial, example comes from the so-called 'Beacon speech' from Aeschylus' play *The Agamemnon* (Appendix 1: 2-4), in which Clytemnestra describes how news of the fall of Troy was brought to Argos overnight by means of a beacon chain. The scene is, of course, mythical and at one time the episode tended to be dismissed out of hand as a poetic fancy (Verrall 1904, XXff). But the speech does go into great geographical detail, identifying each of the relay stations involved, when it could easily have glossed over such matters. It has thus been suggested that Aeschylus would not have dared just to pluck likely positions out of the air and construct a system which at least some of his audience would know to be impossible. His system could thus be based on something real. This might be the beacon chain with which the Persian general Mardonius (Appendix 1: 7) had intended to transmit news of the fall of Athens to king Xerxes at Sardis during the Persian Wars in 480 BC (Hoernle 1921, 14ff); a hypothetical Greek system used to warn of the approach of the Persian fleet at the beginning of the same war (Keen forthcoming and Leiner 1982, 61ff), or a system actually in being in the play's own day (458 BC) when Argos and Athens were allies (Merriam 1890, 17ff and Calder 1922, 155ff). Whatever the case, if Aeschylus really was describing an operational link between the Dardanelles and the heart of Greece, this could be our only complete account of an ancient beacon chain. For, despite the poetic language, most of the positions can now be identified, although a few are disputed (Keen forthcoming, Merriam 1890, Fraenkel 1950, Vol 2, 154ff and Denniston & Page 1957, 94ff) and, although the author has not been able to confirm it in person, a number of writers have stated that the lines of sight are such that the system is theoretically operable (Keen forthcoming and Merriam 1890, 26f).

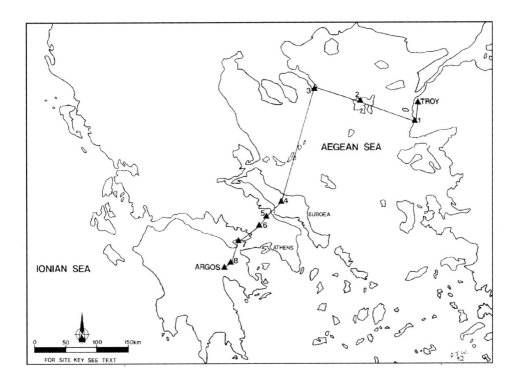

3   *The 'Agamemnon Beacon Chain'.* After Keen

If we adopt the site identifications put forward by Keen, the distances between relays are as follows (**3**):

| | |
|---|---|
| Troy to (1) Mt Ida | 36km |
| Mt Ida to (2) Lemnos | 105km |
| Lemnos to (3) Athos | 70km |
| Athos to (4) Makistos | 173km |
| Makistos to (5) Messapion | 45km |
| Messapion to (6) Kithairon | 33km |
| Kithairon to (7) Aigiplankton | 21km |
| Aigiplankton to (8) Arachnaion | 45km |
| Arachnaion to Argos | 21km |

By far the longest link is the 173km (107 miles) from Athos to Makistos (3-4), which is still well below the American experimental maximum. The two sites are reported to be intervisible (Merriam 1890, 25f), but there are also signs of a gap in the play's text at this point which, it has been argued, may have allowed the name of an intermediate station to become lost (Keen forthcoming, Calder 1922, 157ff, Fraenkel 1950, Vol 2, 155f, Denniston & Page 1957, 96 and Diels 1914, 72). If so, the longest assured link would then be Mt Ida to Lemnos (1-2), which is far below the American maximum at a still respectable 105km (65 miles). In the humid, less transparent air of Britain and Northern Europe, ranges would probably have been somewhat lower, but even here it is not uncommon to see smoke visible at ranges of over 30 miles; thus a beacon could also have been seen from as far. In practice, however, the main limit to a beacon's range is that imposed by the local topography, and it is notable that the two longest links from the *Agamemnon* list were between mountain tops transmitting across water, with nothing but the curvature of the Earth to restrict them. The later stages ran largely overland through sometimes quite rough terrain. Here the views would have been more restricted and the signalling links are consequently much shorter.

In addition to their other strengths, beacons are also more immune to the vagaries of climate than other visual signalling methods, which is why they were also employed as lighthouses in the ancient world. The signal is simple but powerful and thus less likely to become obscured or distorted by poor reception conditions. A bright light can pierce a misty night and still be seen from a surprising distance and, even by day, smoke will stand out from a mist despite its similar appearance, especially as misty air is usually still and so the smoke will not be dispersed. Indeed, fire and smoke are almost always the last things to be visible at a given range when visibility closes in.

Whatever their advantages, however, the limitations of beacon communications are manifest and are largely due to their simplicity. As Polybius points out (Appendix 1: 31), a beacon is largely restricted to giving basic prearranged signals such as 'Danger', 'I am here', 'I am under attack' etc. They are almost incapable of dealing with the unexpected or, indeed, of transmitting anything but the specific message for which they were installed.

Some elaboration is possible, however, and simple codes can be carried by using more than one fire. For example, the English Armada Beacons used a three light code (Kitchen 1988, 2ff and Southern 1990, 236) which read: one beacon, 'enemy sighted off shore'; two beacons, 'enemy look likely to land', which triggered a local muster; and three beacons, 'enemy landed in stronger force than can be handled locally', which launched a more general alert. There are no accounts of such multi-light codes from antiquity, but it is still quite possible to envisage their use. Roman frontier installations, for example, could easily have operated systems in which, say, one light meant 'trouble' whilst two meant 'serious trouble' and, in more general situations, multiple beacons could have been used to signal opposites such as 'advance/retreat', 'Plan A/B', 'Friend/Foe', etc. Nevertheless, useful though they may have been, even these systems could not transmit messages that had not been specifically planned for in advance. Moreover, the information content of a beacon signal might be further degraded by being passed down a relay system, since the point of origin of the message could become hard to determine for a recipient who could no longer see it directly. Some systems would avoid this problem because they only existed to link one fixed point with another, as in the *Agamemnon* example, where the signal could only have come from Troy. But on a Roman frontier, where each garrison fort might oversee a long stretch of the line, containing tens of individual watchtowers, it would be important to know where alert signals originated so that men could be sent to deal with whatever trouble they proclaimed. As a halfway measure, a well-designed relay system might allow a recipient to determine at least the direction from which a signal had come, if not from how far, by arranging that messages coming to a fort from, say, the east were relayed by stations that were also all east of the fort (and vice versa). Yet even that might not always have been either possible or sufficient. In compensation, over relatively short distances, an initial beacon alert could always be supplemented later by more detailed information carried by messenger and we have an ancient reference to just such a duel mode approach being taken by Scipio at the siege of Numantia in 133 BC (Appendix 1: 17). But, again, this would become more difficult as the range increased and on really long systems even messengers sent by the nearer relay stations might not know where a given signal had come from. These limitations could and did lead to confusion, and Thucydides (Appendix 1: 8) describes an occasion in 429 BC when a signal from the island of Salamis, warning of a Peloponnesian attack, was relayed to Athens via its port at Piraeus, causing panic in the city, where the Piraeus relay fire was taken to mean that the enemy were already in the port itself.

The beacon's capacity for confusion and misinformation is further exacerbated by its very inflexibility for, once given, its signals are very difficult to cancel or countermand. We have already seen that the ancients considered war experience important in a signaller, to make him less likely to panic or misinterpret events and so issue false alarms, and medieval records also stress that beacon men should be 'wise, vigilant and discreet' (Kitchen 1988, 7). The larger and more complex a beacon system becomes, the greater the risk of inappropriate signals causing serious confusion. The danger of feeding false alarms into a truly vast system like the English Armada Beacons was such that, in its later days, the express permission of a Justice of the Peace was necessary before any beacon could be lit (Kitchen 1988, 14). The resulting delays did much to rob the system of the speed that was its very *raison d'être* and probably hastened its eventual abandonment. Nevertheless, the precaution was still thought necessary to avoid the chaos and frustration of reversing musters triggered by false alerts and to avoid the danger that people might simply come to ignore a system they knew to cry wolf.

Finally, as beacons would often have been as visible to the enemy as to their intended recipients, their use risked giving away sensitive information. They might, for example, betray a force's position, or rob an attack of at least some of the element of surprise. We have no ancient references to the deliberate imposition of the visual equivalent of radio silence, but we do have one example where normal practice was reversed to deceive an enemy, so that the signal was initiated by extinguishing the beacon (Appendix 1: 23) rather than by lighting it, which suggests that the potential problem had not escaped notice.

Despite its limitations, however, the beacon is the only long-range signalling device whose regular use can be firmly identified in ancient accounts. For although more sophisticated techniques are described in theory, only beacons can be seen actually operating in real historical situations and the uses to which they were put are exactly what we might expect of such a restricted but simple device. They could send recognition signals to distinguish friend from foe (Appendix 1: 42) and allow troop bodies to stay in touch whilst moving separately (Appendix 1: 41). They carried basic news, usually that some anticipated event had actually occurred (Appendix 1: 2-5, 7 and 35). They allowed elementary command and control, usually by giving instructions for prearranged plans to be carried out, and they could help co-ordinate such plans, if only by allowing two or more separate groups to let each other know that each was in position, or simply by signalling, in effect, 'Now' (Appendix 1: 10 & 16). They were also a favourite means of co-ordinating action between siege armies and fifth columnists within a city's walls. Indeed so much so that the Greek writer Aineias Tacticus suggests that even city guards should be forbidden to carry lanterns in case they tried to use them to signal to the enemy (Appendix 1: 12). The beacon's oldest (Appendix 1: 1) and most common function, however, was to transmit alarm signals to warn of an enemy attack and/or to summon help in dealing with it. Here, the signals acted like modern burglar alarms, merely warning of danger, and their low information content was relatively unimportant. Their speed allowed resistance to be mustered quickly whilst more detailed information could often be sent, if more slowly, by messenger.

In addition to the ancient written evidence, it is possible that we may also have at least two Roman artistic representations of beacons, in the opening scenes of the second century AD columns of Trajan and Marcus Aurelius in Rome (**4 & 5**). The relevant section of the Marcus column is less well preserved, but both show a similar scene, with a series of towers along the River Danube, outside one of which stand two conical hay or straw stacks and a substantial log pile. Cichorius (1900, Vol. 2, 20) has suggested that these were beacons prepared for action, with the hay ricks designed to produce smoke plumes by day, whilst the log piles would burn fiercely to produce a bright light at night. But, although the idea has since been repeated so often that it is usually accepted as established fact (e.g. Lepper & Frere 1988, 47f, although see Donaldson 1985, 22f), there are a number of problems with this identification which need to be addressed.

Apart from the obvious fact that this equipment is not shown outside all of the towers, the main objection concerns the log piles, which the columns show as being made up of densely packed and substantial timbers. Experiments by the writer have shown such stacks to be remarkably fireproof, especially as a later scene from Trajan's column shows similar structures being constructed from freshly felled trees whose wood would still be green (Lepper & Frere 1988, Pl 88). Experiments have shown that when green Hawthorn logs (normally an excellent firewood) are stacked like this, they will do little more than smoulder, even with the help of petrol. Older wood does burn rather better, but for timber to ignite easily in such a stack it must be dry and virtually rotten. Moreover, Trajan's Column shows identical stacks in a variety of other uses, such as ballista bases, temporary fortifications and building platforms (Lepper & Frere 1988, Pl's 47, 54 & 98), none of which can be linked with signalling, so that they may represent some form of general purpose, prefabricated structure. Interestingly, however, the column shows the wood piles as having two distinct, alternating layer types (**4**). In one, the horizontal beams are shown passing round the stack, whilst in the other, beam ends protrude from all four sides. This could be an artist's error, but it could also imply that the timbers were stacked in a series of radial patterns separated by spacers. This configuration is particularly good for seasoning wood, as the logs have little contact with each other and an identical stack can be seen in an eighteenth-century German print in exactly this role (White 1989, 179ff & figs 4 & 5). The German timber was seasoned through the winter then rafted down river, as logs may well have been on the Roman Danube, and it is possible that the columns are showing nothing more than wood piles, possibly military supplies, that have been left close to a tower for security.

4   The 'Beacon Scene' from Trajan's Column

5   The 'Beacon Scene' from the column of Marcus Aurelius

The haystacks initially appear more promising, because they would ignite and burn enthusiastically. As Cichorius says, they would produce smoke by day, but they would also generate enough light to make night-time alternatives unnecessary. Indeed, the stacks might have been purposely designed to burn well as they are built in tall columns, apparently arranged around a central supporting timber, and experiments have shown that, with dry fuel, flames will leap up such structures with remarkable ferocity, whilst the central support also acts as a sustainer. Nevertheless, there are problems here as well. The ricks are not shown actually being fired, and so just because they would have made good beacons it does not necessarily follow that that is what they were. For a start, they are built at ground level whilst, as we will see in later chapters, the intervisibilities that made Roman signalling possible were often dependent on the full height of a watchtower. Again, it is also peculiar that only one of the towers shown on each column is equipped with such 'beacons', and a more logical signalling arrangement might have been something akin to a medieval fire basket mounted on each of the tower tops themselves. Even allowing for artistic licence, the hayricks seem unnecessarily large, when a fire basket would burn quite brightly (or smokily) enough for most purposes and they are also both too close together to burn independently, and dangerously close to the tower. On balance, therefore, it seems perfectly possible that the structures are exactly what they seem to be, simple hay or straw-stacks for animal fodder or bedding, and it is worth noting that in the Danube area today modern Yugoslavian haystacks are still built in exactly this way.

White (1989, 187) has pointed out that the soldiers in the tower scenes are wearing cloaks and suggests that the 'hayricks' are really stacks of grain still on the ear, with the apparent central poles actually leather caps designed to keep the topmost ears dry. Taken together, he would argue that these images may have been intended as nothing more than an autumn or winter motif, to imply that the military campaigns commemorated over the bulk of both columns' friezes either started late in the year or, at least, that preparations for them began well in advance. This is less than fully convincing, however, not least because the (albeit damaged) soldiers are wearing their cloaks open and appear to be naked underneath, which is hardly suitable attire for the harsh winters of the Danube lands. Nevertheless, the idea does at least show how open the column scenes are to reinterpretation. All we can really say is that although they may well represent beacons, this cannot be regarded as even remotely certain and past discussions of the issue have probably been more than a little over-optimistic.

If the scenes from the columns are ambiguous, beacons are perhaps the one ancient signalling technique for which we might also expect to find archaeological evidence. Again, however, the situation is currently uncertain, for there are, as yet, no conclusively identified Roman beacons. This is not to say that such beacons did not exist. We can be sure from the ancient writers that they did, and in considerable numbers. Unfortunately, however, their very nature makes them hard to identify archaeologically, as it is almost impossible to distinguish them from ordinary bonfires. Worse still, most excavations of Roman towers only look at the buildings themselves and so miss any external beacons that might have been associated with them. A handful of unusual structures are known which could represent beacon stances, but even these present difficulties and the situation does not seem likely to improve in the near future. For example, a burnt area was found on a clifftop just outside the Claudian coastal fortlet of Martinhoe in North Devon. This has been interpreted as a beacon for communicating with ships at sea (Fox 1967, 20 & fig. 2), but it could just as easily have been a bonfire and there seems to be no stratigraphic proof that it even relates to the Roman period at all. A series of enclosures, expansions and platforms (Hanson & Maxwell, 1983, Steer 1957, Keppie & Walker 1981, 239f and Woolliscroft forthcoming (a)) on the Antonine Wall have also been put forward as beacon stances, but again, the evidence is uncertain. No sign of burning was found at the only excavated enclosure but, although one each of the platforms and expansions have shown evidence of fire, there remains a possibility that these structures may once have supported buildings, which eventually burned down.

Further east, in the Syrian Desert, a number of circular rubble pads (3-10m in diameter) have been found, some of which sit beside towers, and these have also sometimes been seen as beacon stances (Poidebard 1934, Pl's 59, 95-6 & 104). But, although, again, the identification cannot be dismissed outright, their function and date are uncertain and they are not said to bear traces of burning. They are also only one stone thick, which would hardly have raised fires to a more visible height. Yet why else a desert beacon should need a base when its surroundings were neither damp nor flammable remains unclear. The pads could, of course, still have been mounts for some other form of signalling apparatus, which needed a firm foundation but did not produce evidence of burning. But, if so, it seems odd that the equipment was not simply installed on the towers, whose height would give the signals greater range.

In addition to these supposed single stances, two sites have been put forward as multiple beacon positions, capable of operating something akin to the Armada Beacon chain's multi-torch signalling. Unfortunately, however, these are even more doubtful than the simpler installations. The first is at Four Laws (Northumberland) where Sir Ian Richmond (1940, 101f) found a series of seven circular stone standings c.3.3m in diameter and 5.2m apart. Richmond believed that these platforms formed a signal relay between Hadrian's Wall, to the south and its outpost fort to the north at Risingham, but they are very ill-equipped to do so, for the standings are not intervisible with any of the sites they supposedly link together. They are ranged from north to south along the Roman road of Dere Street, rather than east to west as one might expect of a system designed to signal north-south and, as they encroach upon the line of the Roman road, it should have always been apparent that the two were not contemporary. Fortunately, excavation has now settled the issue (Binns 1971) by showing the structures to be relatively modern platforms built so long after the road had gone out of use that 10-15cm of soil had had time to form on its surface.

The second possible multi-beacon site is at Giffa in Syria (Poidebard 1934, Pl's 103-4) on the Roman road to Palmyra, where four somewhat larger standings have been found with two on either side of the road. Again, however, the stonework encroaches onto the line of the road and, whilst proof is lacking on this site, they also seem almost certain to be post-Roman.

The only reasonably convincing excavated beacons are three structures found in association with Watchposts 1/47, 1/56 and 1/57 on the Roman frontier in Germany (ORL, Abt A, Band 1, Strecke 1, 54 & Tafel 13, 16, 21 & 22). They consist of large (20-40cm diameter) post-holes surrounded by a ring of stone packing. It has been suggested that these features were built to carry fires laid round a central support; Southern (1990, 139f) has argued that these fires were designed to illuminate frontier crossings at night. This does appear somewhat unlikely, for the very existence of crossings at this point is conjectural and only the example at WP 1/47 had been fired, whereas one would have expected all of them to have been used repeatedly had they been designed for routine, or even occasional lighting. The original German account argues, more plausibly, that they may have been hayricks with central posts like those on Trajan's column and, if so, one of a number of possible interpretations of their function would again be signalling. This does seem to give a better fit with the excavated evidence, as we might expect beacon firing to be a rare enough event that some sites might never have needed to use them at all. Yet there are problems even here, for the same pattern would be produced by the accidental burning of just one of a number of ordinary hayricks. Moreover, these postholes were almost certainly found by chance. The excavations were conducted by the *Reichslimeskommission* around the turn of the nineteenth century and, as was all too common in that period, the work was often far from thorough. The fact that only one posthole was found at each site is no guarantee that there were no more to be found. The possibility cannot be ruled out, therefore, that they may have formed part of larger structures, rather than being independent entities. As the postholes are undated except that they are stratigraphically later than the frontiers' late second-century earthwork barrier (the Pfahlgraben), they may not even be Roman at all.

## Coded signalling

The ancient world was fully familiar with the use of codes and ciphers to protect written material and a number of techniques were employed including alphabetic substitution and devices, such as the Spartan cipher rod (Plutarch *Lysander*, 19. 5-7 and Aristophanes *Lysistrata*, 990-4), which could physically scramble and then reconstruct written text.[1] Indeed Suetonius (Augustus, 88), commenting on the Emperor Augustus' use of written cipher, finds it remarkable only because the code he used was so simple, merely substituting each letter by the next in the alphabet so that, for example, 'CODE' would become 'DPEF'. It is thus not surprising to find a number of ancient writers describing signalling techniques which attempt to get round the limitations of beacon signals by transmitting multi-message or full alphabetic codes. Such methods would have enormous potential advantages, freeing the signaller from prearranged messages and allowing him to send whatever a particular situation required. An efficient system would allow complex information to be sent much faster than a messenger could carry it, especially when used at long range; even a more cumbersome arrangement might have allowed communications of some sort to be maintained where conditions or enemy action would otherwise have made contact impossible. Complexity can also create problems, however. More sophisticated signalling requires more, and/or better-trained manpower. Alphabetic signalling naturally requires literate operatives (who would often have been less available than today), and complex techniques are also more prone to mechanical breakdown and carry a greater risk of messages being garbled in transmission, relay or reception. Nevertheless, if ancient armies could have mustered the skill and technical refinement needed to make such systems work properly, their advantages would have been manifest.

Unfortunately, unlike beacons, most of the more complex systems are only described in theory by the ancient writers, rather than in operation, which means that we cannot be certain that they were ever put into regular service. Appendix 1 (25-8) includes a number of references to historical signals sent by unidentified systems which must have been capable of more than one message. But the possibility still exists that at least some of the methods for which we have detailed descriptions may have been little more than the inventive imaginings of writers who considered themselves military experts. Such doubts are further strengthened by the apparently eccentric design of the more complex and labour intensive of these methods, and modern scholars, including myself in the past (Southern 1990, 233f, Donaldson 1985, 19ff and Woolliscroft 1989, 9), have tended to dismiss them as unworkable. But experiments conducted for this book have shown that in fact all of the techniques described by the ancients are capable of sending readable signals and so it is still worth looking at each of these methods in detail.

## Synchronised water clocks

This technique is described by the Greek writers Philon, Polybius (quoting Aineias Tacticus) and Polyaenus, with the latter claiming that it was used by the Carthaginians in Sicily (Appendix 1: 49-51). Polyaenus' apparatus is slightly different to the others but all three describe the same basic system. In essence two different signals were sent: the message itself, which was conveyed by the water clocks, and what might be called co-ordination signals, which were sent by torches. The clocks themselves consisted of a water-filled metal or pottery jar, with a corked hole towards the bottom through which the water could be released. Both sender and receiver had such a jar and the writers all stress that these must be identical and presumably filled to the same level. The clocks were calibrated with a series of gradations each of which represented a separate message, and it is here that the only difference emerges between Polyaenus' Carthaginian vessels and the Greek systems of Philon and Polybius. For the Carthaginian jars had the measurements marked on their internal surface, whilst the slightly more complex Greek equivalents had them on a wooden rod protruding from a cork float on the surface of the water (**6**). The Carthaginian clocks were thus read by looking into the jar and comparing the water level with a fixed scale, whilst the Greek ones read off a floating scale against the top of the jar. Experimental reconstructions by the author showed very little difference in the operating efficiency of the two systems so long as there was enough light to see into the vessels. But the Greek system works better at night, where the external scale is easier to illuminate, making the clocks quicker to read and to fill accurately. This is especially true if the scale rod is passed through a wire loop at the mouth of the jar to keep it vertical and provide a fixed sighting line. The Greek scale rods can also be changed to allow for additional messages, and/or periodic code changes.

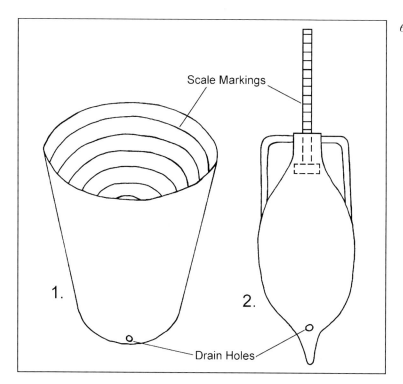

6 *Carthaginian and Greek signal clocks.* After Leiner

To make a signal the sender first showed a torch to alert the receiver, who reciprocated to show when he was ready. The transmitter then lowered his torch and immediately both parties uncorked their jars to allow water to run out. As the water level in the jars fell, different scale markings were passed until the message the transmitter wished to send was reached, whereupon he raised his torch a second time to tell the receiver to replace his cork. As the water should have run out of the jars at the same rate, the level in both should still be identical and the receiver could thus read off the message from his own vessel's scale.

The use of water clocks was well known in the ancient world (e.g. Vitruvius 9, 8, 2ff) but, at first sight, this all still sounds rather Heath Robinson (although I am told that the basic principle is still used today in a German children's game). In particular one might doubt whether the ancient world had the precision engineering skills needed to make the system work reliably. It is in fact surprisingly difficult to make water run out of two vessels at exactly the same rate and even tiny inaccuracies become more serious the longer the clock is left running. The author initially built a pair of clock reconstructions using identical modern plastic measuring cylinders, with the drain holes drilled in exactly the same place on their scales with precision power drill bits. But even given such aids, it took almost an hour to get the two running exactly together and minute filings could make a noticeable difference over the clocks' full running time. It seems unlikely that ancient craftsmen could ever have made truly identical jars and even if they could, they would have found it more difficult to drill them in exactly the same place and with holes of exactly the same diameter. This means that there would inevitably have been inaccuracies in the clocks on which the whole technique depended. To make matters worse, the system does not permit one of the standard checks for confirming accurate signal reception: the reading back of messages by the recipient. For the clock inaccuracies would be consistent and would, therefore, self correct when the message was transmitted back so that the sender would be fooled into thinking that the correct message had been received when it had not. Fortunately, the ancient sources are working from a false assumption. For as the jars simply acted as timers, there was no more need for them to be physically identical than there is for modern clocks. All that is necessary is that both clocks keep the same time and are capable of running long enough to transmit the desired range of messages. This means that, in practice, radically different jars can be used so long as their scales can be calibrated to run to a common time.

Another difficulty with the system is the cumbersome nature of the apparatus as reported in the ancient sources, for the jars described by Philon and Polybius are enormous. Philon specifies a capacity of 150 litres (Appendix 1: 49), whilst Polybius demands no less than 200.8 litres (Appendix 1: 50), and both require scale graduations more than 5.5cm apart. Such formidable dimensions may mean no more than that normal large transport amphorae were to be pressed into service to save the need for purpose built vessels. But as there were smaller containers at least as freely available, they might also have been seen as a safety precaution to minimise the effects of inaccuracies. They would though have made the system very unwieldy to use, both by limiting the portability of the equipment and by increasing its demand for water. Such size would also have lowered operating speeds, especially if more than one signal was to be sent, by making the jars' refilling times longer and possibly also their running times. Again, however, the sources have exaggerated the requirements as, so long as they are properly calibrated, very much smaller vessels can be used with no loss of accuracy or information carrying capacity (bandwidth). For example, the author's initial reconstructions used 600ml measuring cylinders with only 0.3 per cent of the capacity of Polybius's monster jars. Yet these proved consistently capable of resolving scale graduations of as little as 8mm, with 100 per cent accuracy over prolonged periods of use (with a 4mm drain hole), despite the fact that the experimental operators had had no prior practice with the vital torch co-ordination signals. When running, the water level in these vessels fell at an average rate of 3.86mm per second (the rate of flow lessens with time as the pressure at the drain decreases). This equates to a usable time interval of just 2.1 seconds; the accuracy was further increased by the fact that such a tiny drain hole can be blocked and unblocked with the thumb, which is far quicker than a plug and cannot be mislaid.

Similar results were obtained later using rather more realistic apparatus built for the author's appearance on the BBC television series *What The Romans Did For Us* (**7**). These reconstructions were still much smaller than Polybius' jars, at around 57cm high and with 16 litres of usable capacity, but they did use earthenware amphorae with Greek style floating scale rods. Although the vessels themselves were modern reproductions, they should provide a more realistic impression of the handling characteristics of the original equipment. These clocks had a drain hole 1cm in diameter and an average fall rate of 4.58mm/sec. They should thus be capable of resolving scale graduations of around 1cm given the same 2.1 second time interval. This has proven to be the case so long as, once again, a thumb is used to open and close the drain holes whilst the clocks are actually in

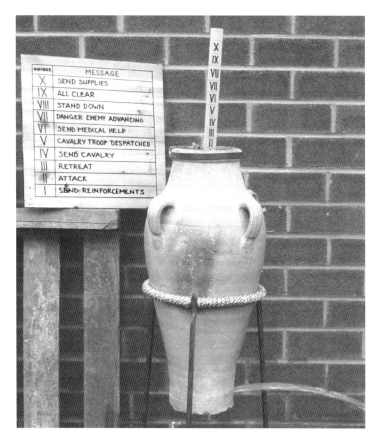

| NUMBER | MESSAGE |
|--------|---------|
| X | SEND SUPPLIES |
| IX | ALL CLEAR |
| VIII | STAND DOWN |
| VII | DANGER· ENEMY ADVANCING |
| VI | SEND MEDICAL HELP |
| V | CAVALRY TROOP DESPATCHED |
| IV | SEND CAVALRY |
| III | RETREAT |
| II | ATTACK |
| I | SEND REINFORCEMENTS |

7  *A BBC water clock reconstruction, running*

operation. The bung specified in the ancient accounts is best reserved for use whilst the apparatus is left standing full.

Furthermore, the bandwidth of these miniature systems was actually greater than that of the Polybian vessels. Polybius states that his jars should be three cubits in height, roughly 132cm which, allowing for a base, a drill hole and the draught of the float, would give them space for between 21 and 22 of the 5.55cm scale intervals specified. The usable scale of a 600ml measuring cylinder is just 19.2cm long, after allowance for the float and drill hole, but with graduations only 8mm long, it still allows for 24 separate messages. The larger BBC reconstructions are more versatile still, for they are long enough to take a scale rod up to 45.7cm long which, with a minimum scale interval of 1cm allows for up to 45 messages.

This leads on to the main shortcoming of the system. The sources regarded each scale graduation as a separate prearranged message and quote examples such as 'send grain', 'send ships', etc. So long as the signaller's needs were met by the repertoire available on the equipment, the system was quick and efficient. The average message during experiments, including the torch signals, took only 20 seconds to transmit with the measuring cylinders, and 30 seconds with the BBC vessels (albeit under drill conditions). Even 21 messages could not cover all eventualities, however, and there would be times when a signal was urgently needed which the system was just not designed to facilitate.

The 24-45 message capability of the reconstructions, however, is sufficient to encode the entire Greek or Latin alphabets. Indeed the longer scales of the BBC reconstructions could encode the alphabet with a much longer, and thus safer, scale interval of 19mm (4.1 seconds run time). It is thus possible to envisage the system transmitting original alphabetic signals, albeit slowly, as an emergency supplement to its prearranged repertoire. This would need nothing more than a modified scale rod and an extra co-ordination or clock signal to announce that alphabetic code was to follow. The transmission speed would naturally be very slow and in experiments even the tiny measuring cylinders could only average two characters per minute, so that a simple message like 'Help' would take around two minutes to transmit. The larger BBC vessels were even slower and it took some practice with them before a speed of one character per minute could be achieved. But this speed could be increased significantly if two jars were used in tandem so that one could be refilled whilst the other was transmitting. The facility may have been useful if range or enemy action made more rapid contact impossible. The sources may thus have underestimated the system's capabilities and if it ever did see actual service in the field, it may well have used smaller, more flexible equipment.

The system's maximum range (terrain allowing) is obviously dependent on the distance at which the torch co-ordination signals can be seen, rather than on the clocks. No experimental maxima have been published for pitch torches, but an attempt by Prof. S.T. Parker to operate the signalling system of a *c.*35km stretch of Rome's Arabian frontier found that they were still clearly visible at a range of 10km (Parker 1986, 83f & fig. 24). The author's own experiments have used rather indirect methods and so although indicative should only be treated as a guide.

During signalling tests on Hadrian's Wall, it was found that even tiny, reflectorless, 6v electric light bulbs could be seen as clear sparks of light at a range of up to two statute miles (3.22km) on a slightly hazy night. A reconstructed Roman torch, consisting of a 15cm band of cotton wool soaked in roofing pitch and mounted on a dowel proved to be almost exactly 64 times as bright as the electric bulbs[2] and although no field tests have been made to prove it, the inverse square law[3] would suggest that the pitch torch should be visible from about eight times further away. This would give it a range of around 16 statute miles (25.74km) on a reasonably clear night, which could probably be doubled by using a larger torch, especially as ancient nights would have been darker than our own, in the absence of light pollution. The system's absolute maximum range in open terrain was probably in the region of 30 miles (51km), on the rare occasions when a transmitting site commanded such a view, which could be further extended by relays. Polyaenus' claim that it was used to communicate between Sicily and Carthage (*c.*125 miles) is hard to believe, however, unless a very much more powerful light source was used, such as a beacon placed behind some form of shutter mechanism.

The system was probably at its least effective during the day and again the co-ordination signals are the limiting factor. Even the brightest pitch flame can only be seen at comparatively close range in daylight and non fire-based signals such as flags and sails are either equally limited, or too slow to be accurate. Smoke signals might just have been precise enough, however, although no experiments have been conducted, and despite its limitations the system should have been usable as an all-day and reasonably all-weather technique.

## Signalling by torch combinations

Another method of transmitting cipher was by torch combinations. We have seen that beacons could combine to send simple codes, but more complex systems which were expressly designed to signal alphabetically occur in the sources. The oldest and most complicated of these was described and, he claims, invented by Polybius (Appendix 1: 47).

Unlike beacons, the Polybian system required a lot of equipment. But, although it can never have been very mobile, it might have been useful on fixed positions. The transmitter consisted of two sets of five torches (designated left and right) which could all be raised and lowered independently. In front of each group was a screen, the height of a man, which hid the torches when not in use and allowed the receiver to see the lights blink clearly on when raised and then out again when lowered. Polybius states that the code itself was carried on a set of five tablets, of which the first carried the first five letters of the Greek alphabet, the second, the second five, and so on up to the fifth which held the last four. The tablet numbers were represented by the lights of the first torch group, and the letter positions on each tablet by those of the second, allowing all of the alphabet to be encoded. This needlessly complicated arrangement can be reduced to a matrix of five rows and five columns which contains the entire Greek alphabet thus:

|   |   | Left torch group (No) | | | | |
|---|---|---|---|---|---|---|
| R |   | 1 | 2 | 3 | 4 | 5 |
| I |   |   |   |   |   |   |
| G | 1 | Alpha | Beta | Gamma | Delta | Epsilon |
| H |   |   |   |   |   |   |
| T | 2 | Zeta | Eta | Theta | Iota | Kappa |
|   |   |   |   |   |   |   |
| G | 3 | Lambda | Mu | Nu | Xi | Omicron |
| R |   |   |   |   |   |   |
| O | 4 | Pi | Rho | Sigma | Tau | Upsilon |
| U |   |   |   |   |   |   |
| P | 5 | Phi | Chi | Psi | Omega |   |

To initiate a signal, the transmitter first raised two torches (perhaps one from each group) to alert the receiver, who answered in kind when he was ready. Once these contact signals had been lowered, the text was sent by the two sets of torches as a series of column and row numbers which could be read off the matrix to spell out the individual letters. So, for example, if we assume that the left-hand group was responsible for the columns and the right-hand group for the rows, the letter Sigma would be represented by three torches on the left and four on the right. Chi would be seen as two on the left and four on the right. When seen from the receiver's point of view, the results would thus look something like this:

Sigma    ★★★    ★★★★
Chi      ★★     ★★★★★

8   *A Polybian*
    *'A'-frame*
    *torch*

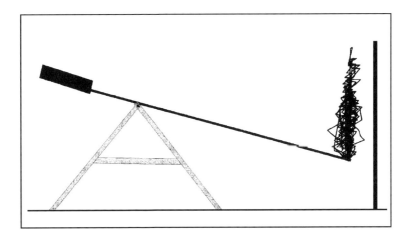

whilst a simple word like 'Lambda' would be seen thus:

| Lambda | ★ | ★★★ |
|--------|-----|-----|
| Alpha | ★ | ★ |
| Mu | ★★ | ★★★ |
| Beta | ★★ | ★ |
| Delta | ★★★★ | ★ |
| Alpha | ★ | ★ |

The matrix could naturally be memorised and (contra Polybius) need not be physically present, any more than an experienced modern signaller requires Morse or semaphore tables. Once received, a message could either be read as clear text or further decoded according to circumstances.

The system has a number of advantages over the water clock method, of which the most obvious is versatility; being specifically designed to carry alphabetic code, it is very much faster at doing so. Just how much faster, however, depends on the method of operation. Polybius does not describe the mechanics of the torches themselves, but experiments by the author have shown that there are two potentially workable systems. The first takes a labour intensive, low technology approach and uses simple handheld torches. These need one man for every two torches which, in practice, means that three men are needed for each of the two five-torch groups (two of which have a torch in each hand), a total of six per transmitter. The second uses less manpower, but requires more complex equipment. Here the torches are mounted on a pivot bar supported by 'A'-frames (**8**), with or without counterweights to make them easier to lift. Each set of torches can be operated by a single man who uses a sliding rod to select how many lights will be raised at a time and, if present, the counterweights should project upwards so that this rod will engage with them to provide a firmer grip. The torches are then raised by pressing down on the rod. The 6-man approach is easier to set up, but Polybius' description reads as though he anticipated the entire apparatus being worked by a single man (Appendix 1: 47). This could be poor use of language or a corruption in the manuscript tradition, but it

*9  The BBC 'A'-frame signalling reconstruction*

could also imply that the system he envisaged was something more akin to the frame-mounted torches. Indeed Polybius' description could easily be read to mean that the same man was expected to transmit from each of the two torch groups in turn. If this type of apparatus was his intention, however, it might be thought that the system's practical value to a real operational army might be questioned, for the bulky equipment would have been cumbersome to transport. In practice, however, it is relatively easy to dismantle and reassemble, or even to improvise from scavenged materials in the field.

The author was long unable to acquire accurate performance data for the frame-mounted system because of the difficulty of building a full-size reconstruction. However, experiments with 20cm wide models suggested that the method works most efficiently when the torch counterweights still leave the beams significantly front (flame end) heavy. Although this makes the lights heavier to lift, they drop back out of sight far more crisply when released than if counterweighted close to their balance point. With practice, the model could achieve transmission speeds of around 20 characters per minute, although this almost certainly exaggerates the technique's potential. Fortunately, however, full-size reconstructions were again commissioned for the BBC television series *What The Romans Did For Us* (**9**) and experiments conducted both during the making of the programme and since have allowed what should be more realistic performance data to be obtained. The BBC apparatus lacked counterweights and used heavy planks rather than poles to hold the torches. As a result, it is probably slightly slow to operate, but the difference should not be great and the limiting factor may have been the speed at which signals could be read accurately, especially at any distance, rather than the rate at which they could be transmitted. After a little practice, transmission speeds of up to 12 characters per minute could be coaxed from these reconstructions and slightly faster speeds might be possible with modified equipment and more training. This compares surprisingly well with the models, and a transmission speed of 10-14 characters per minute is probably a realistic rating.

The six-man approach also proved able to send 12 characters per minute in experiments, but, with inexperienced operators, the test data is probably again a little on the pessimistic side. For although the light handheld torches can be raised and lowered very quickly, more training appears necessary with this approach to produce a well co-ordinated crew. Polybius stresses the need for practice when using the technique, and a well-drilled transmitter detail could probably have improved on our own rather amateur efforts without much difficulty. Whichever approach is used, however, optimal speed can only be realised if none of the actual signallers are expected to read the text being transmitted. Both methods benefit from having a separate caller to shout out the text, bringing the final transmitter crews to three or seven. Where each of the torch operators knows the code table it is enough to just call out each letter in turn but, failing that, calls such as 'Right one, left three' or, better still, 'One, three' do not measurably slow the transmission rate.

Whatever the exact bandwidth of the Polybian system, a transmission speed of around 14 characters per minute makes it many times faster than water-clock signalling. It could be argued that the clocks were never designed to transmit alphabetically and might still send their standardised messages faster than the Polybian system could spell them out. But this might not be true, for it should be remembered that the Polybian apparatus does not exhaust its capacity in encoding the entire Greek alphabet. The 10 torches together are capable of 25 separate signals, one more than the alphabet needs, and the spare '10 light' code could be useful for system signals or error codes. It could, for example, be used to mean 'Word ends' or 'Message ends', but it could also have signalled a change of transmission mode from letters to set codes. If this were done the system would have the capacity to transmit 24 separate prearranged messages (with the 10 light position kept free), which is more than is claimed by the ancients for water clocks, and probably much faster. The spare code could also be used to check reception accuracy for, if the receiver read back the signal by copying each torch combination as it was made, the 10 light position could be used as a correction signal meaning something to the effect of 'Error, watch again'. Additionally, alphabetic signalling itself could be used to spell out abbreviated messages, such as the many three letter codes used in Morse, the best known of which is obviously the distress signal 'SOS'.

Despite its advantages, however, the system has a number of weak spots. Some could be overcome, but others must have lowered its usefulness to a point where one wonders if it could ever have had more than marginal military value. The possibility (at least) of complex and cumbersome equipment has already been mentioned, but two other problems still remain to be looked at.

The first and more minor is lateral inversion, the phenomenon whereby one person's left becomes right for anyone facing them. This has obvious implications for a system where the decoding process depends on the ability to differentiate between left- and right-hand transmitters. For the sender's right would become the receiver's left and any uncertainty as to which was which would cause chaos. The problem could, in fact, be overcome fairly easily by using separate transmitter and receiver codes with left and right reversed. Although this does not seem to have occurred to Polybius, two aspects of his text suggest that he was aware of the problem and put thought into correcting it. Firstly, he hints that the two sets of torches should signal separately, with the left-hand lights being raised first, presumably to reinforce their identity. Indeed, at the cost of halving the transmission speed, it would be perfectly possible for just one torch set to send column and row information alternately, albeit at the risk of causing confusion should either the transmitter or receiver personnel lose their place. More interestingly, however, he states that both sender and receiver should be equipped with a double *dioptra*. This is a Greek optical surveying instrument akin to a theodolite, which measures angles by moving a sighting barrel against calibrated horizontal and vertical scales. A detailed description has survived in the writings of Heron of Alexandria (3, 187-315) and this has allowed modern reconstruction attempts. Perhaps the most convincing is that produced by Dilke (1971, 75ff & fig. 19), but although only a single mounting, this is a complex and bulky piece of precision engineering which can hardly have been mass produced, given the technological limitations of the ancient world. Therefore it can never have been routinely issued to the multitudinous signalling sites of systems such as Roman frontiers. Nevertheless, a double *dioptra* would deal effectively with lateral inversion because an instrument with the two sighting barrels crossed could artificially reverse the phenomenon, giving sender and receiver the same left and right.

The Dilke *dioptra* is a precision surveyor's tool which would have been expensive and slow to produce because it needed to be accurate. But no such precision is needed in a signaller's aid and it would have been a waste of machinery to use such a tool when perfectly adequate instruments could be made far more cheaply. Figure **10** shows an example built by the author. It is made from just six rough sawn pieces of wood. It cost £1.50 in materials and took only 20 minutes to build. Again only a single mounting, it consists in effect of a gun sight, with ring fore and back sights mounted at opposite ends of a sighting arm. The arm is held by a cradle which allows it to swing up and down to measure elevation against a vertical scale that is held by a steering arm mounted beneath it. For lateral readings this entire sighting assembly rotates round a screw attached to a tripod mounted base plate with a horizontal scale on its surface that is read against the side of the steering arm. It is, without doubt, a crude piece of engineering. Yet it has consistently proved to be accurate to within 25 arc minutes, both vertically and horizontally, which is more than enough for signalling purposes.

Interestingly, it is not hard to think of other uses for *dioptras*, especially in Roman frontier signalling. They would, for example, provide a way of determining the origin of signals sent at night. Figure **11** shows the vertical and horizontal scales of my own reconstruction, which are calibrated, not with degrees, but with the bearing of every Roman installation visible from a particular site. The position, in this case, was the Roman tower of Barcombe A, behind Hadrian's Wall, near the fort of Vindolanda, but any other installation could easily have a similar instrument calibrated for its own field of view. The advantages of such a device are that it can be aimed towards any incoming signal and

*10 The author's* dioptra *reconstruction*

identify the installation transmitting, or it can be accurately aligned in advance on any site from which a signal is expected, even in total darkness, all by using the scale calibrations. This could be useful in its own right, but it would also be a formidable weapon against attempts at jamming or deception.

Only two ancient references to the jamming of fire signals have come down to us, both of which describe the same incident during the siege of Plataea in 427 BC (Appendix 1: 29 & 30). But these do, at least, make it clear that the concept was known in antiquity. Fire signals, and especially beacons, are vulnerable to two distinct forms of external tampering. The first operates rather like modern radio jamming, with an enemy lighting spurious fires near a particular line of sight, to mask genuine signals which may then pass unnoticed. The second is more akin to computer 'hacking' where an enemy attempts to enter the system himself. Here he may modify or countermand legitimate signals, as in the Plataean example or, for psychological warfare purposes, induce false alarms as a diversionary tactic or to put nervous and physical strain on defenders and bring them to distrust their own system. In a static and closely knit entity like a Roman frontier such attempts would probably have been futile by daylight when the site garrisons would have had the installations of their sector in view, but at night one might easily be fooled by such tactics. Yet, although there is no written or archaeological evidence for the use of such devices on frontiers, a primitive instrument, such as the author's *dioptra* reconstruction, would be sufficient to thwart such attempts. For, unless the jamming lights were put on

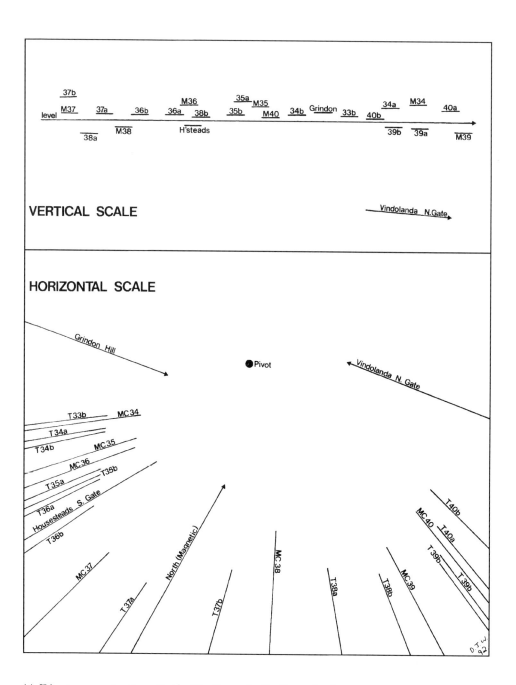

11 Dioptra *reconstruction, site identification scales for Barcombe A tower*

exactly the right line of sight, it is quite accurate enough to pick out the presence, or absence, of even a faint genuine signal from within a cloud of spurious fires. Its ability to identify sites would also allow it to check whether or not an isolated signal was coming from a legitimate position. Indeed, the *dioptra* may have satisfied a general need to check up on apparent incoming traffic on ancient signalling sites, as in addition to deliberate hostile action, fire signals can be jammed accidentally by a wide range of perfectly innocent light and smoke sources.

To return to multi-torch signalling, however, the system's most serious difficulty is its range. Unlike the co-ordination signals of the water clock method, the range of this system is not determined by the ultimate distance at which the torches can be seen, but by the distance at which the different lights can be separated by the unaided eye.

If two identical lights are placed side by side and looked at from progressively greater ranges the eye will eventually fail to resolve them and they will appear to fuse into one. In field experiments the (somewhat longsighted) author could just resolve lights (modern battery torches) placed 2m apart, from 3800m ($2\frac{3}{8}$ miles), which equates to an angular resolution of *c*.1.8 arc minutes. This allows us to calculate a theoretical maximum range for the Polybian system, for we are given the size of the torch groups. Polybius states that the screen in front of each five-torch group should be 10 Roman feet (2.96m) long. Allowing 20cm between the outermost torches and the edges of the screen, to ensure they are properly hidden, this leaves 256cm for the remaining three, an overall spacing interval of 64cm. Given a 1.8 minute optical resolution, this is only enough for a maximum range of 1200m and then only if the lights are kept equally spaced, something that would be difficult to achieve consistently with the six man, handheld torch approach. Experiments with the BBC reconstructions suggest that this theoretical range is probably about right. These torch groups were built 20cm narrower than Polybius specifies to allow them to fit into a vehicle for transport but, although this will inevitably have reduced their capability, the difference should not be great. Certainly they still remained perfectly usable when tested at a distance of about 1km during filming (on this occasion carrying flags and not torches for daytime operation). Nevertheless, at ranges of more than about 700m transmission speeds would need to be lowered slightly to make sure that signals could be read with confidence. The ancients lacked any means of magnification, but this range could still be extended by moving the torches further apart. This can only be done within limits, however, for the larger the torch groups become, the slower, more difficult and more manpower-intensive they would be to operate. At a range of 3800m each torch group would already be 8.4m long, by which point it would have become impossible for one man to work two hand torches (or one whole 'A'-frame group). This would necessitate 11-man transmitter crews and, at the maximum torch range of *c*.30 miles, both torch groups would extend over a minimum of 102m, meaning that the transmitter as a whole could barely be shorter than 300m if a reasonable separation between the two groups is allowed. This is too long for the letter-caller's voice to cover reliably, especially in less than perfect conditions. Indeed the need for such a control mechanism would probably have been one of the principle limiting factors, so that in practice the system's maximum practicable range was probably no more than two to three miles. At this distance its transmission speed would still have given it some advantage over a mounted messenger, but the range would fall further in misty or turbulent air, possibly dramatically so. It is also hard to envisage the system in action at even this range by daylight, for although the BBC apparatus worked perfectly well at *c.*1km using flags, these could not have been seen at 2-3 miles. Any boards or smoke plumes that might be substituted for them would be slow and cumbersome to operate. Finally, the transmitters would have been both too long and too manpower-intensive to have been used on small fortifications such as the towers of a Roman frontier and one again wonders to what extent the technique would ever have been of much practical value.

There is, however, a variant on the Polybian multi-torch system which might work rather more effectively, and this simpler technique is reported by the third-century AD writer Julius Africanus (Appendix 1: 48) to be both highly impressive and in use with the Roman army of his day. It uses just three torches, designated left, right and centre, which encode a third of the alphabet each, with each torch being responsible for eight letters. The system uses varying numbers of flashes of the individual lights, rather than combinations of different lights to transmit letters so that one flash on the left signals 'alpha', two flashes 'beta' etc., until omega is signalled by eight flashes on the right. An alphabetical code table for the system would thus look something like this:

| | | Light | |
| No. of flashes | Left | Centre | Right |
| --- | --- | --- | --- |
| 1 | Alpha | Iota | Rho |
| 2 | Beta | Kappa | Sigma |
| 3 | Gamma | Lambda | Tau |
| 4 | Delta | Mu | Upsilon |
| 5 | Epsilon | Nu | Phi |
| 6 | Zeta | Xi | Chi |
| 7 | Eta | Omicron | Psi |
| 8 | Theta | Pi | Omega |

and the word 'Lambda' would now appear as:

| Letter | Left | Centre | Right |
| --- | --- | --- | --- |
| Lambda | | ★ ★ ★ | |
| Alpha | ★ | | |
| Mu | | ★ ★ ★ ★ | |
| Beta | ★ ★ | | |
| Delta | ★ ★ ★ | | |
| Alpha | ★ | | |

Such a system has a number of advantages over the Polybian method. It requires less equipment than the 'A'-frame version of the 10 torch technique and is, therefore, much easier to set up, whilst using less manpower than the hand torch variant. Its range is increased, as the torches need only be about 25m apart to be separated by the naked eye at the extreme *c.*30 mile visible range of the lights. As a transmitter only 50m long could probably still be controlled by the voice of a letter-caller, this potential increase in range should have been fully usable. There would also be no need for additional personnel with distance as each operator was already responsible for only one torch. Smoke signals could probably be substituted for the torches in daytime and the technique would impose few transport overheads since it can be operated far more quickly with light handheld torches and a screen, which could easily be improvised on the spot.

As each character now requires an average of four signals, one would expect the technique to be markedly slower than the Polybian system but this is not really the case. Experimentation by the author has shown that the system can still send *c.* 10-12 characters per minute and this could be further increased by rewriting the code table to the Morse standard so that the most commonly used letters are assigned the least number of flashes. Reception accuracy can still be checked by the receiver copying the transmitter's movements and there is spare capacity for transmitting system messages and error codes as two or more torches can be used in combination.

The system's only real drawback is a more acute version of the lateral inversion problem seen earlier. As described by Africanus, the transmitter would only ever be showing one light at a time. Thus the receiver, instead of having to work out which of two visible torch sets is left and right, has the far harder job of identifying individual distant, but closely spaced, lights as they appear. This is a very real problem and the fact that three separate torches are used means that a *dioptra* would give little assistance, because although triple-barrelled versions would be possible, if cumbersome, the observer has only two eyes to look down them with. At short range it might be possible to use three dimmer lights as position markers for each of the torch positions. At longer ranges these markers would need to be as powerful as the signalling torches to be seen at all, and might not be able to stand far enough from the main lights to be resolvable as separate. This would mean that the effect of raising a signal would be merely to double the apparent intensity of an already visible light. It is an unfortunate psycho-optical fact that it is far easier to see a light flash on and off than just to see it vary in brightness. In the parlance of modern communications, such a system might thus have too poor a signal to noise ratio to be reliable. One possible aid would be to use a modified single-barrelled *dioptra* with a foresight consisting of three adjustable vertical hairs which could be separately aligned on the transmitting lights as part of the contact procedure. Experimentation by the author, however, suggests that the best solution is simply to run the system in the opposite way to that specified by Africanus. If each of the torches is held aloft and visible when not signalling it can serve as its own position marker. Signals would then be made by lowering the relevant torch behind a screen, so that a signal flash would actually consist of one torch momentarily blinking out, whilst the other two remained visible to remove any doubt as to which was in use. Lateral inversion can then be cured by using separate transmitter and receiver codes, with left and right reversed, or even by the senders simply turning their backs on the receivers to create a common left and right, although the latter method does make the checking of reception accuracy more complicated.

The system shares one further disadvantage with the Polybian method, which would lower its value in specialised circumstances such as Roman frontier signalling. For again, a multi-torch transmitter must be spread over a reasonably wide area for its separate lights to be resolved at any great range. This means that it cannot always be mounted on a tower, for the restricted width of a Roman tower top (*c.*3.5-4.5m) would restrict its range to a maximum of *c.*4km. In many instances this might be enough and in others additional range could be gained by signalling from ground level. Yet, as we shall see in later chapters, frontier communications were often wholly dependent on the ability to signal from the full height of a tower and at ranges of up to, and even over, 10km.

## Semaphore

Both the fourth-century Roman author Vegetius and an anonymous Byzantine writer mention signals being made by waving various objects (Appendix 1: 45 & 46) in a similar manner to modern semaphore flags. In the Byzantine case the objects in question are kept vague and could be no more than battlefield standards, but Vegetius describes something much more substantial: a tower mounted beam which is moved up and down to transmit. Unfortunately, he does not provide any further details and, to a modern mind accustomed to two flag semaphore, it is initially hard to see what information such a simple system could convey. It is possible to envisage different beam positions, or different modes of movement carrying different meanings but, as the eye cannot resolve subtle nuances of either from any great distance, this would give the technique a very limited repertoire. We might, for example, imagine the beam being rotated around a pivot like a clock-hand, so that different angles would convey different meanings. But this would allow little flexibility as it is unlikely that attitude changes of much less than 30 degrees (five minutes on a clock face) could be reliably followed from any great range. After all, this is why clocks have two hands, despite the help given to the eye by the face scale, when in theory only the hour hand is strictly necessary. It restricts the beam to just 10-12 message positions, one of which would have to be left as a rest angle. The same applies to using movement. The beam could be moved in at least five different modes: circles, side to side, up and down, and two different diagonals, but much more than that would probably also be over-ambitious.

If we free ourselves from such preconceptions, however, it takes little thought to show that, with simple movements, the beam could become a powerful information carrier, for the system is ideally suited to sending binary based codings like Morse.[4] It is interesting that Vegetius says specifically that the beam should move up and down for, whilst this could just be vagueness in describing more complex movements, it would make a great deal of sense if it was intended to be taken literally.

To send binary code with a beam, a signaller has two basic choices of movement. With Morse, for example, he can either move it right for dot and left for dash (or vice versa), or up for dot and down for dash (or vice versa). The left to right motion is physically slightly easier even if the beam is properly mounted and counterweighted, but it once again suffers from lateral inversion and might confuse an unwary recipient. Vertical motion is immune to this problem, since up and down remain constant, and such a system can send alphabetic code at high speed. In experiments, the author was able to use an unmounted and un-counterweighted 4m levelling staff to send Morse at speeds of up to 20 characters per minute, and for an experienced operator, using better equipment, significantly higher rates, perhaps approaching 30 characters per minute, are probably not unrealistic. This makes the technique potentially the most powerful we have seen and, as the beam can also carry a light, it can function in darkness as easily as by day.

Unfortunately, the system has a surprisingly short range. It is true that semaphore systems have been used for quite long distance signalling in more modern times, but they were always dependent on telescopes. The Romans had only the naked eye and, in experiments with a light on a 4m beam, the author has found that, even in clear air, the movements could only be reliably followed at distances of under 2km (*c*.1½ miles). Naturally this could be improved upon, for a longer beam can be used to give greater travel. But there are limits to how long even a well-mounted beam can become because, as well as being slow and unwieldy, a long beam may flex which makes it more difficult to swing crisply as well as introducing noise into the system. It will also require a disproportionately massive mounting, not just to support its weight, but also to prevent the apparatus being destroyed whenever the beam is caught by a gust of wind.

Another improvement is to raise the beam off the ground and it is noteworthy that Vegetius tells us that the system was used from towers. The author's experiments were conducted at ground level so that the beam could only swing through 90 degrees. This gave it a travel roughly equal to its own length, but in theory a tower-mounted beam would have 180 degrees of travel, equal to double its length. In practice, this maximum would almost certainly be somewhat curtailed by the mounting, but although it would restrict the technique to fixed installations, tower operation would still give a significant boost to its range. The author's experiments showed (especially at night) that the beam's movements were most visible when made crisply and in the vertical plane only, and a well-designed mounting, with the beam carefully counterweighted to its balance point, would thus further increase range as well as improving transmission speed. It is also helpful, at night, if a stationary marker light is deployed as a reference point against which the signal light can be seen to move. By day, the beam itself can be seen and so the recipient is not just left trying to detect the movement of a light. This also gives a certain increase in range, which can be further enhanced if the beam is made more visible by being projected from the tower at right angles to the observer, especially when this leaves it silhouetted against the sky. This may explain why some Roman towers, such as Barcombe B (Woolliscroft, Swain & Lockett 1992) near the fort of Vindolanda, are so accurately aligned to face likely target sites. As beacons and normal torch signals are not affected by orientation, this might in turn be a hint that Vegetius' method was actually put into use. Certainly, there are artistic representations of Roman towers carrying torches on projecting beams, notably on the opening scenes of the columns of Trajan (*see* **4**) and (in less well preserved form) Marcus Aurelius (*see* **5**) in Rome (Lepper & Frere 1988 and Caprino 1955). Although there has been an attempt in recent years to dismiss these as, in effect, lamp-posts, to illuminate the tower's surroundings (Southern 1990), they are at least as plausible as signalling apparatus. Indeed they may even have fulfilled both roles. Moreover, both the two sculptures and Barcombe B date to the second century AD which means that the system may be centuries older than Vegetius.

The technique's range can also be boosted by increasing the sensitivity of the receiver. For, although the Romans had no means of magnification, a great deal can be achieved by further use of the *dioptra*. When trying to detect tiny relative motions of a distant light it is again helpful to have a fixed reference point against which it can be seen to move. It was exactly this principle that enabled the discovery of the Planet Pluto,[5] and it can greatly assist movement perception in the unaided eye. Simply watching a light through a *dioptra* will restrict the field of vision to a tiny enclosed area inside which any motion will become more apparent, even without magnification, especially if the sights can be locked in position to prevent them moving even slightly themselves. A still greater improvement can be gained at night by fitting the foresight with a horizontal cross hair and aligning it so that the signal light will pass above and below it. Alternatively, the sights can be aligned so that the light will actually pass out of the instrument's field of vision altogether at the top or bottom of its swing.

Even these refinements have their limits, however, and it is unlikely whether, combined, they could have done much more than double or possibly triple the system's maximum range, which would thus be confined to about 5-6km, in clear air. Yet, whilst this would not be sufficient to make the system viable for really long range signalling, it would be enough to cope with most (although not all) of the more local watchtower to fort communications of a Roman frontier. Its equipment is simple and relatively compact. It is tower based (and towers are an all but ubiquitous feature of Roman frontiers) and, within its limitations, it works well.

## Other methods

At least three other methods of long range signalling are either mentioned or hinted at in the ancient sources, but the references are vague and their usefulness is hard to evaluate.

### Flare signalling

A single reference in Julius Africanus (Appendix 1: 51) mentions signals made by throwing batches of fuel onto a fire to make it flare up and produce a blaze of flame by night and a sudden plume of smoke that would be clearly visible by day. Africanus' description is unclear as to the workings of the system and we have no way of telling how much, if at all, it was used, but the method would be simple to operate and should also have had a reasonably long range. It appears to have been another method of coaxing beacons to send simple codes. But, although its capacity would inevitably have been limited, Africanus tells us that it could be used to send estimates of enemy numbers by flaring once for every thousand spotted. Other simple messages would also have been possible and information might additionally have been sent by varying the size, frequency and duration of the flares, paralleling the use in modern radio communications of amplitude, frequency and pulse density modulation. A further variant, not mentioned in the sources, would be to produce colour codes by exploiting the ability of certain chemicals to change the colour of a flame. Copper compounds, for example, will turn a fire a brilliant green and, like any metal-working culture, the Romans must have been aware of these effects. Africanus, however, makes no mention of any such possibility and we have no way of knowing if it was ever attempted.

## Heliographs

There are a number of ancient references to daylight signals being made with shields (Appendix 1: 32, and Xenophon Hellenica II, 1, 27) and in one case the shield is said to be gilded (Diodorus Siculus, XX, 51). It is perfectly possible that these are simply short range battlefield communications where a shield was raised or waved to make a signal that might otherwise have been made using flags or standards, but there is also a chance that we are looking at use of the heliograph. If so the ancients would have had access to a powerful long-range signalling tool. Nineteenth-century experiments by the U.S. Coastal and Geodetic Survey (Merriam 1890, 25f) found that, in ideal conditions, a 12in mirror could transmit readable signals to a range of 190 miles (305km).[6] Although ancient polished metal mirrors would probably have been rather less reflective than their modern silvered glass equivalents, their range should still have been impressive. The heliograph is light and fully portable. It is capable of transmitting signals of any degree of complexity and, although less than reliable under northern conditions, it would have been ideal for the Mediterranean World and especially for Rome's Eastern and African desert frontiers. Unfortunately there are no unambiguous references in the sources and no mirror fragments have ever been found on ancient signalling sites (although, as they would have been made of — possibly gilded — bronze and hence valuable and difficult to lose, this is hardly surprising). Thus we simply do not know if the technique was used in the ancient world.

## Pigeons

The only ancient reference to the use of carrier pigeons is a strange story in Frontinus' *Strategemata* (Appendix 1: 44). This does not involve homing pigeons, but describes a Roman attempt to communicate with a besieged city by attaching messages to starved birds and releasing them in the hope that they would fly into the town to seek food. Nevertheless, the fact that such an apparently bizarre idea should occur to anyone may be a hint that the true homing pigeon was known to the Romans, even if none were available on this occasion (or at least none that would home on the required target) and a substitute had to be improvised. If so, they would have made perfect vehicles for communications, for pigeons can fly fast and to tremendous ranges. They can carry written text and, unlike all the other methods discussed, they are totally independent of visual lines of sight. Their only requirement is a fixed base on which to home, something readily available in the fixed dispositions of Roman frontier systems, although less so to an army in the field. It seems likely that most Roman frontier communications would have been between minor observation positions, such as watchtowers, and their parent forts, so that birds would only need to be kept at the forts. It would have been perfectly easy for tower crews to take one or two out in a basket when they went on duty. Again, however, we simply cannot tell whether this was ever done for there are no ancient sources to tell us and, as yet, there is no archaeological evidence for pigeon lofts in Roman forts.

# Notes

1   The text was wrapped around a rod and cut into a spiral shred. This was sent to the intended recipient who could reconstruct it by winding it around another rod of the same diameter. The rods thus acted as de-scrambling keys which could be changed periodically.

2   To compare the two, each was allowed to illuminate a sheet of paper from exactly 30cm and the reflected light was measured by a camera light meter set to a film rating of 400 ISO. The bulb gave a reading of $\frac{1}{15}$sec at f2, whilst the torch registered $\frac{1}{15}$sec at f16.

3   The apparent brightness of a light falls at the square of its distance, so a light needs to be four times brighter if the maximum distance at which it can be seen is to be doubled.

4   Morse is not strictly a true binary system as three positions are needed: dot, dash and silence, but the beam could easily be given a park position as well as two signal positions.

5   Pluto was found by flicking between identical telescope pictures, separated by a time interval, for an object that moved in relation to the fixed backdrop of stars (Simon 1969, 92ff).

6   Surprisingly, Parker's (1986, 84) Arabian experiments referred to above found heliograph signals to have an effective range of only 5km, but his mirror size is not given.

# 2 Hadrian's Wall and the Stanegate

## Background and study area

The basic anatomy of Hadrian's Wall is so well known that it should need little detailed reiteration. Suffice it to say that in its final form the frontier consisted of a 76 mile stone wall, up to 10ft thick (although the western 31 miles were originally built of turf) and of unknown but greater height than the 11ft of the tallest section that still survives. It ran the entire length of the relatively narrow Tyne-Solway isthmus from Wallsend, on the northern bank of the Tyne, east of Newcastle, to Bowness on the southern shore of the Solway (**12**). It was fronted by a substantial 'V'-sectioned defensive ditch and backed by both a road and a massive earthwork, now known as the Vallum, which consists of a flat-bottomed ditch, flanked on either side by parallel earth ramparts (**13**). At one Roman mile intervals along the line the Wall was pierced by gateways guarded by small fortlets which we call milecastles. These divide the frontier into a series of neat divisions or Wall miles and between each milecastle was a pair of watchtowers or turrets. As the milecastle gateways probably also carried towers, the Wall was thus provided with a screen of observation posts set at one third of a Roman mile (493m) intervals. Finally, at spacings of between four and seven miles, the Wall carried a series of large (3-9 acre) forts to house non-citizen auxiliary units of 500 or 1000 men. The Wall did, however, pass through a complex series of modifications before reaching its final form and a number of aspects of this sequence will become relevant as this chapter progresses.

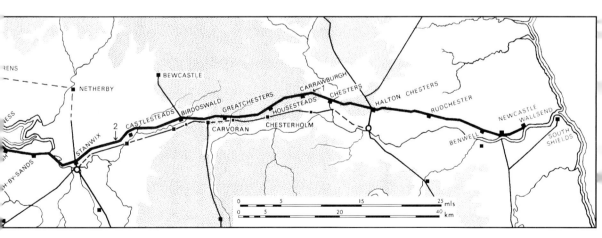

*12 Hadrian's Wall.* D.J. Breeze

*13 Hadrian's Wall at Cawfields, with Milecastle 42 and the Vallum.* Photo G.D.B. Jones

To create a field programme of manageable size, a sample study sector was chosen of about one third of the whole frontier. The sector finally selected was the 28 Wall mile stretch between milecastle 30 at Limestone Corner and milecastle 58 at Irthington (**12**, arrows 1 & 2), and this was picked for three main reasons. Firstly, it is relatively clear of modern woodland, so that the site intervisibilities are reasonably easy to check. Secondly, it is the sector in which the Wall's anatomy is most fully understood, so that the archaeologist can be more confident of having most (although possibly not all) of the original installations available for study. Thirdly, it contains almost all of the terrain types through which the entire system runs, ranging from fairly flat desolate moorland in the east, to rugged crags, and finally softening out into the rolling pasture lands of the Irthing and Eden valleys.

It should also be pointed out that the use of imperial measurements was retained throughout this particular study. This is highly unusual in modern archaeology where the metric system is now almost universal, but as the original spacing data for the Wall was exclusively published in yards it may make comparisons easier if I continue the tradition. Metric equivalents will be given from time to time and maps will be given both metric and imperial scales but, otherwise, the distances given can be easily converted at the rate of 1 yard = 0.9144m.

## The Stanegate

Once the study sector's intervisibility data had been gathered, it soon became apparent that it only made sense if the, perhaps less well known, idea of a frontier on the Stanegate road was first accepted. This system may have existed just to the south of Hadrian's Wall and pre-dated or, in its final form, perhaps been contemporary with the building of the Wall (Breeze and Dobson, 2000, 16ff, Dobson 1986 and Hodgson, 2000). Controversy still surrounds the exact date, form and even the very existence of the Stanegate as a formal frontier line. But the general consensus, at least amongst the system's supporters, has been that as the Roman army pulled out of Scotland during the reigns of Hadrian's predecessors, Domitian and Trajan, this previously unremarkable highway (but see Poulter 1998) began to acquire an increasingly militarised appearance. By the beginning of Hadrian's reign, it may have become a powerful frontier system in its own right, whose size and complexity is only now becoming apparent.

For many years the Stanegate and its associated military works were only thought to have run from Carlisle in the west to Corbridge (**14**). But in the last few decades a number of major new finds have been made on the Tyne-Solway isthmus, mainly by aerial photography, which have caused this view to be reassessed. In the east a large, multi-period fort has been detected at Washing Well Whickham on the south side of the Tyne valley (McCord and Jobey 1971, 120 & Pl. 12). At South Shields, what may be Trajanic levels have been revealed beneath the later fort and stores base (Frere 1986, 375). In the west, the existence of the fort long suspected to lie at Kirkbride on Moricambe has been confirmed (Bellhouse & Richardson 1982). A number of wholly new sites have been discovered including watchtowers at Easton and Far Hill along with two forts to the south of the Wall fort of Brough-By-Sands, one of which overlays yet another new tower (Jones, 1982, 283, Higham & Jones 1985, chapter 2, Esmond Cleary 1995, 342). The road itself has also been seen in this sector and, in places, appears to have been fronted by a defensive ditch and/or palisade (Woolliscroft & Jones, forthcoming). A number of these sites have also now produced Trajanic datings and it appears increasingly possible that the Stanegate, like the Wall, ran from coast to coast.

Only in the central 20-mile sector between Old Church Brampton and Vindolanda, however, is the Stanegate system anything like fully understood. But in this area, at least,

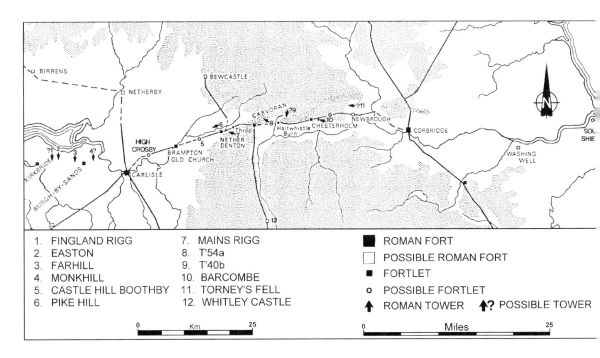

1. FINGLAND RIGG   7. MAINS RIGG
2. EASTON          8. T'54a
3. FARHILL         9. T'40b
4. MONKHILL        10. BARCOMBE
5. CASTLE HILL BOOTHBY  11. TORNEY'S FELL
6. PIKE HILL       12. WHITLEY CASTLE

■ ROMAN FORT
□ POSSIBLE ROMAN FORT
▪ FORTLET
○ POSSIBLE FORTLET
↑ ROMAN TOWER    ↑? POSSIBLE TOWER

*14 The Stanegate System.* After Breeze

*15 The fort of Vindolanda, with the Stanegate road in the foreground.* Photo G.D.B. Jones

*16 Haltwhistle Burn fortlet (1) and the Stanegate (2), set amongst a group of Roman temporary camps.* Photo G.D.B. Jones

the frontier in its final form seems to have been made up of four elements that together form a fairly regular pattern. Along the road itself was strung a series of large, turf and timber, auxiliary forts at roughly seven-mile intervals. Four of these are included in the study sector: Old Church Brampton, Nether Denton, Carvoran[1] and Vindolanda, and as the recent Vindolanda roster tablet has shown, these may have had unusually large garrisons (Bowman & Thomas 1991, 62ff).

Between each pair of forts was a much smaller fortlet, a little over three-quarters of an acre in size, cutting the intervals between major installations to about three and a half miles. At present, only two such sites are known with certainty, at Throp, between Nether Denton and Carvoran, and at Haltwhistle Burn (**16**), between Carvoran and Vindolanda. There is strong aerial and field evidence for a third at Castle Hill Boothby, between Old Church Brampton and Nether Denton (Simpson 1934, 154f and E. Birley 1961, 140).

Finally, and most importantly for the present work, the Stanegate could be linked together by a signalling chain. Some of the forts are actually intervisible, but the rest are connected by a series of watchtowers and it is noteworthy that, unlike most Roman frontiers, these do not occur at frequent intervals to form an observation screen, but only where a signalling link between two major sites is required. The signalling system, over the study sector, thus ran as follows: Old Church Brampton and Castle Hill are intervisible. Castle Hill is linked to Nether Denton via a tower on Pike Hill (they are not

*17 Turret 45a*

intervisible as reported in Simpson and McIntyre 1933, 271ff), which was later incorporated into the Wall as an extra turret. Nether Denton is connected to Throp by means of a tower at Mains Rigg. The remains of a stone tower immediately to the east of the later Wall fort of Birdoswald suggest that Nether Denton also had a forward observation post to supplement its otherwise very limited view to the north. Carvoran, despite a splendid general view to the west, is obscured from Throp by a bold ridge of Thirlwall Common. It was thus also dependent for its communications on a tower which was again later incorporated into the Wall, as Turret 45a (Woodfield 1965, 162ff, which adequately dismisses claims made against the tower in Crow 1991, 62) and which also served to link Carvoran with Haltwhistle Burn in the east (**17**).

Only the link between Haltwhistle Burn and Vindolanda now remains unknown. Vindolanda is situated in a broad hollow with a limited view to the east and only slightly better visibility to the west. But, like Carvoran, it has a closely associated signal tower, which stands three-quarters of a mile to the east on the commanding ridge known as Barcombe Hill. Unfortunately, not even Barcombe can see Haltwhistle Burn, so there must have been a second relay tower to link the two. It has usually been assumed that this lay somewhere on the long hill known as Seatsides (*see* **32**), just to the west of Vindolanda (E. Birley 1961, 147), over which the Stanegate road itself runs, since this ridge stretches almost the whole way to Haltwhistle Burn. But extensive field walking on the hill has failed to find any point that could see both Haltwhistle Burn and Barcombe simultaneously, even from the full likely height of a Roman tower. A more probable site would thus have been the western summit of Winshields Hill just to the north, which at 1250ft was later to become the highest point on the whole of Hadrian's Wall and which offers a splendid view of both sites.

The ideal point on the hill would have been the site of Wall turret T 40b. This has the double advantage of having a vastly better view to the north than Seatsides, giving it a valuable forward observation role, and of being one of the few places able to see both Haltwhistle Burn and Vindolanda directly. Signals sent via a tower on this site would thus not need relaying by Barcombe. It is interesting to note, therefore, that when T 40b was excavated in the 1940s (JRS 1947, 168), it proved to be somewhat larger than a standard Wall turret (as is T 45a) and, although it cannot be proved since the full results of this excavation were never published (and no records can now be traced), it is just possible that, like Pike Hill and T 45a, T 40b was originally a Stanegate signal tower that was later incorporated into the Wall.

Outside the study sector things are much less certain, although we will return to the areas between Old Church Brampton and Carlisle, and between Vindolanda and Newbrough later. In the east almost nothing can be said about potential signalling links for, so far, the forts of Corbridge, Washing Well and South Shields stand alone with no sign of any accompanying fortlets and towers. Indeed, even the course of the road is unknown, assuming that it even reached this far. In the far west, however, there is now sufficient data for the beginnings of a pattern to be discerned, although this seems to be very different from that on the central sector, as no fortlets have yet been discovered. Instead, the forts of Burgh by Sands I and Carlisle are both intervisible with a point at Monkhill (NY 342585) where a faint penannular crop mark on an air photograph taken by the late Prof. Barri Jones (pers. comm.) may show the remains of a signal tower, largely destroyed by a modern building. Professor Jones also detected a faint ring feature some 800m further east at Kirkandrews-on-Eden (NY 350585), at a point with a better view of Carlisle and intervisible with Monk Hill, which may be another tower. The tower underlying Burgh I fort can also see Monkhill and is particularly interesting as it would presumably reflect an earlier period in the Stanegate's development in which the forts were further apart. Further west still, Brough by Sands I is intervisible with a tower on the prominent rise of Farhill (NY 562582), which is itself intervisible with the westernmost tower currently known at Easton. Finally, Easton itself could have been linked with the coastal fort of Kirkbride by means of a tower on Fingland Rigg (*c*.NY 2657), a superb observation position, which also has the more southerly fort of Old Carlisle in view (*see* **41**). A tower at this point would also explain the apparently odd position of Easton, which is situated further north than one might have expected, on low ground beneath the ridge along which the Stanegate itself seems to run, and thus suffers from a very much more restricted field of view. This situation would simply become an economy measure because, as presently sited, Easton is able to see around the north side of a bend in Fingland Rigg to that part of the hill which also has Kirkbride in view. Yet the ridge top to its south, despite its higher elevation, does not have this view and so yet another tower would have been needed to link the two. Sadly, however, if there was a tower on Fingland Rigg, it remains undiscovered, for a likely crop mark, which lay on the ideal signalling spot, has now been found, by excavation, to be a native farmstead (Richardson 1977). For the moment at least, it remains unclear how (or indeed if) Kirkbride was linked to the rest of the line.

## Hadrian's Wall

The Stanegate frontier was essentially an invasion defence depending on large, auxiliary unit-sized concentrations of force that could be combined to form a single substantial army. But, whilst the road itself would, no doubt, have been patrolled and the fortlets and towers would have allowed at least reasonably tight surveillance, the Stanegate was still a very open frontier (except for the palisaded sections in the west). It would have been quite easy for small raiding parties, smugglers, subversives and the like to enter and leave Roman territory unobserved, especially at night or in poor weather. The construction of Hadrian's Wall itself, in the AD 120s, should probably be seen, therefore, as little more than a way of creating a more intensively policed line. It would combat these low intensity threats, whilst causing the minimum further dispersal of manpower, albeit with a propaganda element brought about by its sheer scale. This is all the more so when we consider that, as initially conceived, the line consisted only of the Wall itself and its attendant milecastles, turrets and ditch. For both the Wall forts and the Vallum were slightly later additions and it is important to remember that the Wall was planned and to a large extent built on the assumption that the invasion defense would continue to lie in the Stanegate forts, which were all a little way to its south. The Wall was, therefore, initially intended to be only a thickening of the original system and not a replacement for it.

A number of features of the Wall's design and layout have long puzzled its students. Firstly, the system's builders usually went to great lengths to occupy the most commanding ground, for example by overcoming the enormous engineering difficulties of building a substantial stone wall over the violent undulations of the Whin Sill ridge. Yet the Wall sometimes follows a weak tactical line when stronger ground was available close by. Just as perplexing, if less well known, however, is the curious positioning of some of the milecastles. Although the only ancient literary reference to the building of Hadrian's Wall states that its purpose was 'to separate the Romans from the Barbarians' (Anon, Hadrian, II, 2), Hadrian's Wall was no Berlin Wall and it was never designed to be uncrossable. It was vital that the army could move through it freely for interception and simple maintenance purposes. But it may also have been intended that civilian traffic, trade and, perhaps, transhumance could continue and it was the milecastle gateways that allowed these movements. They were frequent enough for the Wall to offer no serious inconvenience, yet secure enough to allow close scrutiny of travellers, to oversee trade and other movements and to collect the import and export duties that provided an appreciable part of the Empire's revenues. It is, therefore, all the more puzzling to find that a number of milecastles are so sited that their north gates front directly onto the tops of precipitous cliffs, whilst others are only accessible with difficulty. Indeed the recently excavated MC 35 (Haigh and Savage 1984) stands at the top of such a massive cliff that it simply never had a north gate, only a blank wall. What is still more perplexing is that these milecastles often have usable passes very close to them which were ignored.

One explanation, that may be appealing at first sight, is that Hadrian's Wall was a classic example of the inflexible 'You are not paid to think' attitude supposedly prevalent in the military in all ages. The Wall could have been built to a neat plan drawn up by someone with a tidy mind but little or no knowledge of the terrain. This plan demanded milecastles at exact mile intervals and was then slavishly followed no matter how inappropriate it turned out to be on the ground. Militarily, however, the Romans were not fools. Had they have been they would not have won and then ruled a continental empire for more than half a millennium. We must always be careful, therefore, to study the reasoning behind apparent oddities in their military planning before dismissing them as irrational, and this argument does have a decisive weakness, of vital importance to the present work. This is the simple fact that the milecastles are not set at regular, let alone Roman mile, intervals (**18**). They are often close, but although a plan has definitely been closely (and perhaps sometimes inappropriately) followed, some leeway seems to have been allowed (Collingwood 1930).

Despite its rather primitive equipment, Roman surveying could be extremely precise (Dilke 1971) and, if the milecastles had been intended to be at exact one mile intervals, we could expect them to be so sited, certainly to within a few yards. A Roman mile was 1618 yards (1479m), but in the area studied not one milecastle is 1618 yards from its neighbour and only three are within 20 yards of this figure. On the other hand, three are over 180 yards out and one, MC 41, is more than 230 yards (210m) from its measured mile point. In all, the average milecastle is 70 yards (64m) off position.

It could be suggested that this may only serve to inform us that Roman surveying, whilst notoriously accurate as to direction, was less so on distance. But further study of the statistics would appear to refute even this. For although there is a total range in the deviation of milecastles from their measured mile positions (i.e. the difference between the longest and shortest Wall mile) of 440 yards (402m), the average milecastle spacing is one Roman mile and three inches, an amazingly small inaccuracy rate of just 0.000072 per cent. The length of the study sector as a whole is only two yards out over 28 Roman miles (41.4km) of some of the most difficult terrain in Britain. Under these circumstances, only the smallest of the spacing deviations can safely be put down to bad surveying and we are left to conclude that, within limits, the milecastles have been deliberately sited. In a few cases the reason for the deviation is obvious. For example, both MC 38 and MC 48 would have had streams running through them in their measured mile positions, whilst MC 45 would have been set on a rather dramatic split level. But, in other cases, the theoretical position offers a much better building site than the one actually chosen and we must look for another, more general, explanation.

For example, bearing in mind the clifftop sites mentioned above, it might be suggested that milecastles were being moved up to better defensive and lookout points. But a number of milecastles have actually been moved down from the heights into much lower positions. For instance, the measured position of MC 39 (**19**) would have placed it right on the summit of an independent peak at the eastern end of Peel Crags. This site presents a spacious flat building platform. It enjoys a magnificent 360 degree field of view and stands at the top of a range of cliffs so sheer that they are now an attraction for mountaineers. Yet the Romans chose to build the installation 89 yards (81.4m) to the east in the deep hollow known (after it) as Castle Nick (**19**). Here it has a very much more restricted field of vision,

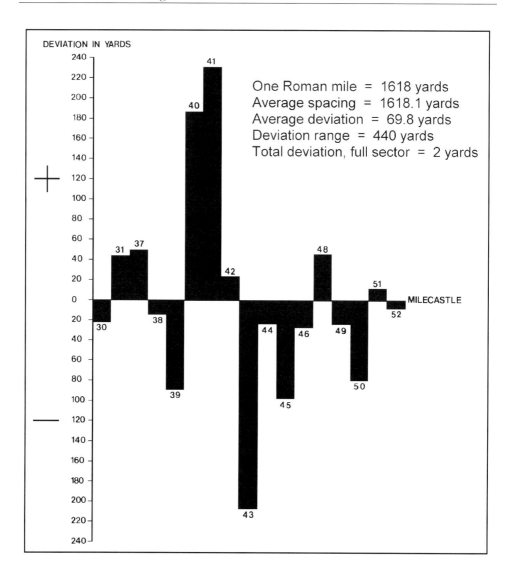

*18 Graph to show the deviations in milecastle spacings from one Roman mile*

especially along the frontier to the east and west and is far more accessible and so less defensible. Likewise, the measured position of MC 41 lies at the top of the westernmost spur of Winshields Hill. Here, at 1200ft above sea level, it again offers strong defences, a splendid all-round view (stretching as far as the Solway in good weather), whilst still providing a suitable flat building platform. Yet the milecastle was built 232 yards (212m) to the west on much weaker ground and with again a more limited field of view.

Alternatively, then, we might wonder whether these sites were being moved to positions specifically chosen for their improved access, to facilitate the fortlets' role as transit points. But here the very opposite problem arises, for a number of milecastles,

*19 Milecastle 39*

whose measured positions lie in passes, have been moved to higher, less accessible ground. For example, the measured position of MC 43 lies at the bottom of a small pass 200 yards (183m) to the west of the later Wall fort of Great Chesters, a pass that now carries two different field roads. Yet the milecastle as built actually underlies the fort. A much better example, however, is MC 53. The measured position of this installation lies in a splendid pass created by the valley of the Banks Burn, a natural route which now carries one of the few direct north-south roads through the area. Yet the fortlet was built on a site halfway up Hare Hill to the west which, although not particularly steep, is so awkward to ascend that the modern farm road has been forced to run up the hill in the Wall ditch.

Just as interesting is the way in which some milecastles were not re-sited as one might have expected them to be if access was a prime consideration. The best examples of this are two of the clifftop sites and probably the most visited milecastles on the Wall, namely MC 37 at Housesteads and MC 42 at Cawfields (**13**, **20 & 21**). Both installations have, in fact, been sited a little to the west of their measured mile positions (by 50 and 23 yards respectively) and in both cases this has obviously been done to improve their accessibility. They have been moved from measured positions where their north gates would have fronted onto the tops of sheer cliffs (**20 & 21**, arrow 1), to sites where the cliffs break up just enough that, whilst the ground is still too steep for wheeled vehicles, access on foot is possible (**20 & 21**, arrow 2). Thus the milecastles as built were usable. Yet both milecastles have bold passes a little to their west (**20 & 21**, arrow 3) which would have made them accessible to any form of traffic and the pass at MC 42 is indeed used today by both a farm road and the visitor footpath. But although we have seen the Romans

20  Milecastle 37

21  Milecastle 42, from Cawfields Crag

prepared to build milecastles over 200 yards from their measured mile points, and although MC 37 and MC 42 would require deviations of only 130 and 55 yards respectively to put them into these passes, the Romans failed to take advantage of the potential and the passes were ignored.

## The signalling system: Stanegate fort phase

One remaining explanation would seem to be that the milecastles were sited for signalling purposes. If so, then quite considerable adaptation of the line has been allowed for signalling and the milecastle spacing deviations might, therefore, hold clues as to how the system functioned. To understand their significance, however, three basic questions must be answered: to whom would the Wall installations have been signalling? How would they have done it? And to what end? The answer to the first question is, in fact, fairly obvious. A Wall installation faced with trouble would have wanted to summon help from the nearest concentration of force, in other words from the nearest fort. At the time the Wall was built, this meant from the forts on the Stanegate, which might lie anywhere from a few hundred yards to a few miles to the south. A great deal of ingenuity has been used by some scholars in the past in trying to devise a means of signalling laterally along the Wall (Selkirk 1987). Puzzlement has been expressed by others at the impossibility of doing so, because the milecastles and turrets are not always intervisible with their neighbours. In practice, however, there would have been little point in having such a system because, initially at least, the lightly manned Wall had nothing on it worth signalling to and it seems probable that signalling would have been oriented to the south.

The second and third questions are rather more difficult. We have seen in chapter 1 that the Romans had access to a number of methods for sending complex messages along visual signalling systems and it can no longer be denied that some of them would have worked. But, in the context of Hadrian's Wall, they may often have been less than reliable, if only because the climate of the area means that visibility is often poor. It seems possible, therefore, that signal traffic on the Wall might generally have been both simple and infrequent, with most detailed messages being carried by courier; this is not to deny signalling an extremely valuable role.

In emergency conditions time becomes important and any time saved is precious. When a Wall installation came under threat it would probably have dispatched a messenger to the nearest fort with news of the exact situation. But a simple beacon lit at the same time would instantly have given the fort's garrison two vital pieces of information. Firstly, they would know there was trouble and, secondly, because the signal was visual, they would be able, at least potentially, to see at a glance exactly where that trouble was. The result would be that instead of having to alert a resting unit the messenger could arrive at the fort to find its garrison already on a combat footing, or even meet it on the move. Not only would the time thus saved be considerable, it would increase in proportion to the distance between the troubled site and its nearest fort, which would go some way towards minimising the potential weakness of the extremities of a fort's sector of responsibility. Such a signalling system would also have had other

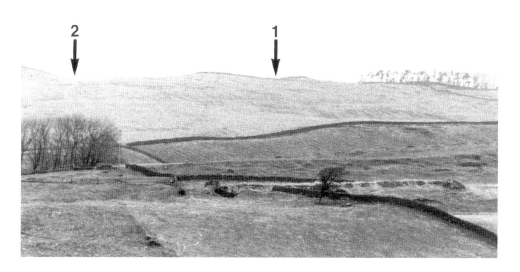

*22 Milecastle 37 from Barcombe*

advantages. For example, it would be very simple to operate since all that would be necessary to transmit would be the lighting of a pre-prepared beacon of some sort, something that could easily be done by the normal Wall garrison without the need for specialist signal men. The dangers inherent in more complex systems, of messages being garbled in transmission, reception or relay, would also disappear and the system can even be argued to have had a potential deterrent effect because its operation would have been extremely conspicuous. It is usually assumed that all military signalling must be carried out in secret. But, in an essentially defensive system, there are advantages both in flaunting the existence of detection apparatus to the enemy and in making sure that he knows when he has been detected. Modern burglar alarms exploit exactly this principle. The sight of Roman signal beacons flashing across the landscape, coupled to a knowledge of the speed and strength of response of which the frontier defenses were capable, must have been distinctly sobering to any cross-border raiding party not already deterred by the very existence of the system.

The question to be answered, therefore, is: are the deviations in milecastle spacings consistent with an attempt to fit the Wall with a comprehensive signalling system oriented to the south? The answer would appear to be yes. It is immediately apparent from even a cursory inspection of their remains that Wall installations tend to have a good view to the south, even in those sectors that have limited views to the north. Secondly, the six milecastle oddities already cited are all explicable in terms of this theory. The data suggest that the Romans did indeed try to site milecastles in accessible positions, to maximise their usefulness as transit points, but that, ultimately, their need to signal took priority over any other consideration.

*23 Milecastle 42, from Haltwhistle Burn fortlet*

For example, **22** shows a telephoto picture of MC 37 (arrow 1) as seen from Barcombe and it can readily be seen that if the milecastle had been sited in its adjoining pass (arrow 2), it would have been hidden behind a rocky spur and would thus have lost contact with the signal tower, which linked it with the fort of Vindolanda. Likewise, had MC 42 been built in its pass, it would have lost its current direct link with the fortlet of Haltwhistle Burn because this pass is obscured from the fortlet's view by a spur of the now much quarried Cawfields Crag (**23**, arrowed). So although the Romans did their best to provide some access to these installations, the otherwise superior pass sites had to be foregone.

The situations at MC 43 and MC 53 are identical. These milecastles should, as already stated, have been sited in passes simply on spacing grounds. But, once again, these positions were not in visual contact with Stanegate installations and both fortlets had to be located on sites where signalling was possible. MC 43 was moved east to a position visible from Haltwhistle Burn and MC 53 was moved west to a point intervisible with Castle Hill Boothby, a fact that might in itself be taken as further evidence for the existence of that fortlet. Where milecastles could be made more accessible without compromising signalling, however, the Romans took full advantage of the opportunity and this is the position at MC 41 and MC 39. MC 41 was moved down Winshields Hill into what is, in fact, the lowest piece of flat ground still visible from Haltwhistle Burn (**24**, arrowed). The re-siting of MC 39 in Castle Nick was a dramatic improvement made possible only because from full tower height the site is still, just, intervisible with Barcombe.

Signalling would thus appear to have been given an absolute priority, even over the prime function of the milecastles, and the Wall's design was adapted accordingly. There does, however, seem to have been a limit imposed on these spacing deviations. For example, to build MC 35 in a position where it could have been both accessible from the

*24 Winshields Hill, from Haltwhistle Burn fortlet*

north and still in visual contact with the nearest Stanegate site (in this case Barcombe) would have necessitated a full third of a mile deviation to the site of T 34b and so the fortlet was left on its cliff with its north gate omitted.

Signalling also seems to have taken priority over some tactical considerations, because some of the odd lines already mentioned as taken by the Wall can also be explained in terms of the need for Wall/Stanegate intervisibility. The prime example here is the sector between MC 49 above Willowford and MC 52. Throughout most of this stretch the Wall clings to the very edge of the north side of the Irthing valley. But at close range to the north is a ring of hills which, while enjoying commanding views themselves, completely obscure the Wall line's own view north. The extra work required to take in these hills would have been negligible in terms of that expended on the system as a whole, while the tactical benefits and improved outlook would be considerable, yet the hills were ignored. The explanation is that the Wall, at this point (here the turf Wall), is already running along exactly the most northerly line visible from the fort of Nether Denton and its signal tower at Mains Rigg. Indeed only the turret and milecastle gate tower tops would have been above the skyline as things were. With the Stanegate here running near the bottom of the steep sided Irthing valley, the tactically superior ground to the north, despite its higher elevation, is simply out of sight and so could not be used.

The final test, however, must come from the full intervisibility data. If the Wall was designed around a comprehensive, Stanegate-oriented signalling system, one might expect all Wall installations, both milecastles and turrets, to be directly intervisible with a Stanegate fort, fortlet or signal tower. If the terrain made this impossible, they should at least be sited so that the signals of any one blind installation could be relayed to the Stanegate by a neighbour. And this is exactly the pattern indicated by the data (**25**). If we

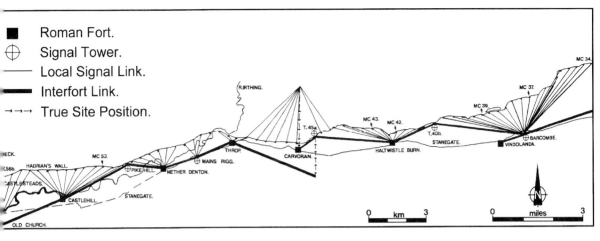

*25 The signalling system of Hadrian's Wall: Stanegate fort phase*

ignore, for the moment, the first four miles of the study area, from MC 30-4, whose Stanegate sites are unknown, all but one of the 72 remaining Wall installations studied are in direct visual contact with a Stanegate site, despite very difficult terrain, whilst the only exception, T 56b, can be easily relayed into Old Church Brampton via its neighbour, MC 57. Furthermore, the data would seem to indicate fairly clearly defined spheres of responsibility, with each Stanegate installation overseeing a particular length of Wall.

It would, therefore, appear that Hadrian's Wall did have an efficient and comprehensive signalling system in its initial phase, at least within the study sector. The Wall itself can be seen more clearly than ever to have been merely an adjunct to the Stanegate frontier, around which it has been very carefully tailored. The skill with which the Wall's designer has grafted this highly complex addition onto a system that was probably never designed to receive it is remarkable and his, sometimes sorry, reputation needs to be reassessed.

This is not the end of the matter, however, for having used known sites on a well understood part of the Wall to discover the signalling system, it began to appear possible that the process of investigation could be reversed and an understanding of the system itself be employed in a search for new sites on a less well understood sector. It cannot be stressed too highly that what follows is conjecture, but the results proved interesting nonetheless.

The idea was first used in an attempt to explain the lack of direct intervisibility between T 56b and a known Stanegate site. At first sight this lack of contact may appear unimportant. The turret is the only Wall installation tested to have no direct Stanegate link and even it has a simple one-stage relay to the Stanegate fort of Old Church Brampton. Unfortunately, the situation is more serious because it would, in fact, have been perfectly simple to give T 56b a direct link to Old Church and the very line of the Wall in the turret's vicinity appears to show a flagrant disregard for both Wall/Stanegate intervisibility and, indeed, any feeling for tactical good sense. On the two mile sector from MC 56 (Walton) to MC 58, Hadrian's Wall follows what is tactically an absurd line (**26**). Instead of running over the bold hill that later carried the Wall fort of Castlesteads, it follows a route round the north of the hill and along the valley of the Cambeck. In doing so it puts itself at a threefold disadvantage. Firstly, the line is longer here than it need have been. Secondly, the Wall faces steeply rising ground immediately to its north, which, in places, reduces its view to a matter of yards, while rendering its defensive position untenable. Finally, the line of the Wall puts Castlesteads Hill between itself and Old Church Brampton, cutting off T 56b's direct signalling path. Castlesteads Hill is so obviously a superior position that the Wall can only have avoided it for a reason. The hill has fine, all-round visibility and its sheer north face is all but impregnable. Yet its other sides, especially the south and east faces, are more gentle and would have presented no technical difficulties to the Wall builders. The only explanation might be that there was already something on the hill when the Wall was built and, as a minor installation, like a tower, would simply have been incorporated into the line in the manner of Pike Hill, that something can only really have been Castlesteads fort.

Although Castlesteads was virtually obliterated by eighteenth-century landscaping, excavation (Richmond & Hodgson 1934) has shown that below the stone Wall fort are traces of an earlier turf and timber fort. Because Castlesteads lies on the turf sector of Hadrian's Wall, it might be assumed that the turf fort belonged to this early turf Wall phase, while the stone fort was part of the general process of replacing the Wall itself with stone. But the possibility exists that the turf fort at Castlesteads may pre-date the Wall altogether and might, instead, have formed part of the Stanegate, whose forts are also of turf and timber. At first sight this does appear unlikely because of the close proximity of the known Stanegate fort of Old Church Brampton, less than two miles to the south, and because Castlesteads lies at some distance from the Stanegate road. But if Castlesteads can be re-dated then the problem of T 56b disappears, because Castlesteads is in direct visual contact with T 56b along with every other Wall installation on the MC 56-8 sector. It can also see the Stanegate sites of Old Church Brampton, Castle Hill Boothby and Pike Hill, and the Wall's signalling system, in the study sector at least, would thus be left pristine, with every single Wall installation, without exception, directly linked to a Stanegate site. Moreover, if Castlesteads did originate as a Stanegate fort, its reuse as a Wall fort is not without precedent. For the fort at Carvoran also remained in use and, here again, the Wall was run a little way to its north, whilst the purpose-built Wall forts are all attached to the barrier.

If knowledge of the signalling system could be used, however, tentatively, to explain an anomalous site, it seemed possible that it could also be used to prospect for completely new ones. To test this idea, an attempt was made to locate the fortlet that should lie between the Stanegate forts of Carlisle and Old Church Brampton. Two basic rules of thumb which had emerged from the field-work were of considerable help in this search. Firstly, each Stanegate site tends to be at the extreme eastern limit of view of its western neighbour, and secondly, the Wall tends to be built along the northern limit of view of the Stanegate.

The furthest point east along the Stanegate that can be seen from Carlisle is a tiny hamlet, almost exactly halfway to Old Church Brampton, called High Crosby. The most likely fortlet site appeared to be at the highest point, on a small hillock (NY 455600) just to the north of a modern farm (**27**). The site lies immediately to the north of the Stanegate Road and has an excellent view of the Wall line, especially to the west. It is not

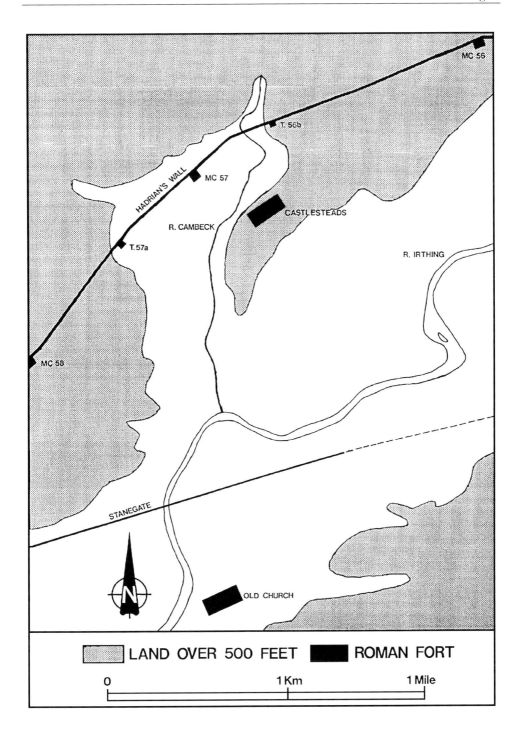

26  *Map of Castlesteads and its vicinity*

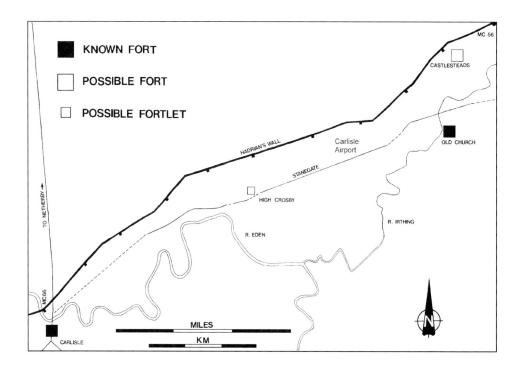

*27 Possible Stanegate sites between Old Church Brampton and Carlisle*

intervisible with Old Church, but a link could have been provided by just one tower, in the northern part of what is now Carlisle airport, possibly in the vicinity of the modern control tower. From here it could have overseen the small section of Wall not directly visible from either High Crosby or Old Church. If proved to exist, these sites would extend the sector in which every known Wall installation is intervisible with a Stanegate site at least as far west as MC 63. No such sites have yet been found, but this is still a rather promising result because, when the Stanegate was first traced through High Crosby (Simpson, Richmond, Hodgson & St Joseph 1936, 182), early second-century Roman pottery was found in its ditches at exactly this point. This suggested to their excavator that there had been settlement nearby and led her also to predict the presence of a fortlet, in this case under the farm.

With this encouragement, a second experiment was conducted, this time from Barcombe Hill. The furthest point east along the Stanegate that can be seen from Barcombe is a farm called Grindon Hill (**28**) and, again, a fortlet has long been suspected to lie at this point, mainly on spacing grounds as the farm is three and a half miles from Vindolanda. The farm can see the Wall line and it is also the point at which a Roman road to Housesteads leaves the Stanegate. Indeed, Grindon Hill is the first point east for some distance that does have a view of the Wall because for about a mile to its west the Stanegate's view to the north is blocked by a broad ridge. Unfortunately, excavations designed to find a fortlet here have failed to find any trace and, in recent years, doubts have

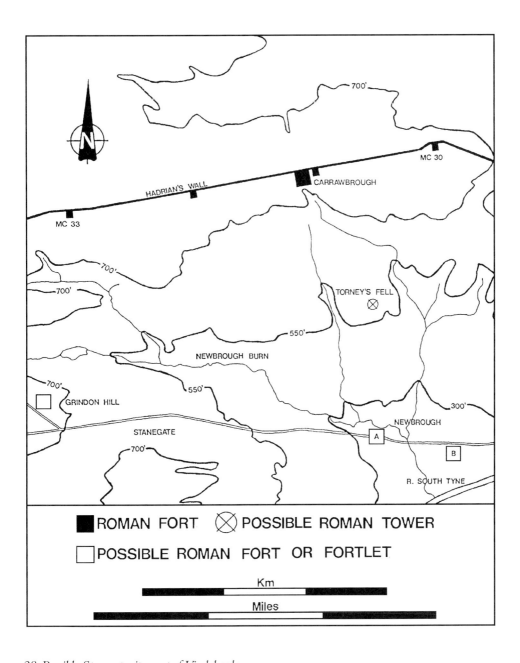

*28  Possible Stanegate sites east of Vindolanda*

been cast on the need for such an installation in this rather desolate spot. However, the methods used here would predict that the fortlet did not lie under the farm at all, but on a low (sadly much quarried) hill about 300m to the north-west, where no excavation has ever taken place (NY 823683).

In the sector between MC 33 and T 34a, Hadrian's Wall runs for some distance with higher ground at short range to its south, so that Barcombe's view of it ends at MC 34. It would, however, have been easy to extend this tower's area of responsibility to the east, simply by running the Wall a little to either the north or the south of its actual line. In view of the negligible amount of extra work required, the fact that this was not done suggests that something else was able to take up responsibility for the Wall at the point where Barcombe loses sight of it and this can only really have been the Grindon Hill fortlet. Grindon Hill Farm loses contact with the Wall just to the west of MC 33, leaving almost a whole Wall mile blind. But the more northerly hill site boasts a view that overlaps with Barcombe's by over a mile. It may therefore prove a stronger contender than the traditional location to be the fortlet site, despite its rather greater distance from the Stanegate road, especially as it also occupies a better tactical and lookout position.

The next suspected Stanegate site to the east is at Newbrough, where a fourth-century fortlet is known to underlie the Church (Simpson 1930). The traditional Stanegate model predicts that this small village, three and a half miles east of Grindon Hill, should contain a full cohort fort and, although the continuation of this model cannot be relied on, there are, at present, two candidates for the fort's location. The first, Newbrough A (**28**), is the church yard, where an earlier fort may yet await discovery beneath the fourth-century structure (especially as much reused material was found in its structure). The second, Newbrough B, is a field about a third of a mile further east (NY 878678) where a series of crop marks have recently been discovered from the air (Jones 1991) which resemble a Roman fort or, more probably, a marching camp. Neither site has any great advantage over the other and no attempt will be made here to chose between them. What can be done, however, is to try to link any fort that may have existed at Newbrough into the signalling system. Unfortunately, as Newbrough lies in a pronounced hollow beside the South Tyne, neither fort site can see Grindon Hill and neither is in contact with the Wall, so that a fort here must have been dependent for its communications on nearby relay towers.

Any signal tower serving Newbrough must fulfil three basic criteria. It must have a good view of the Wall line. It must be visible from Grindon Hill and it should be able to see at least one and preferably both of the Newbrough fort sites. It might also help if it had a good view to the east to continue the system still further. The only place that meets all these requirements is a desolate hill to the north of Newbrough church, called Torney's Fell (NY 868696), and if there was a tower linking Newbrough to the rest of the Stanegate it would almost certainly have been here. Sadly, although unploughed, the fell has been badly scarred by modern drainage work, making a ground search difficult. One candidate site has been detected in the form of a low mound raised slightly above the general level of the moor and, unlike its surroundings, well drained (**28**). But, although a number of stones protrude from the mound's surface, they form no discernible pattern, and a resistivity survey by the author gave no clear results so that, for the moment, the existence of a tower here remains no more than a hypothesis.

Torney's Fell is also intervisible with the Wall fort of Carrawburgh, however, and this fort is known to overlie an earlier, rectangular, turf structure (Breeze 1972). Amongst a number of possible interpretations offered by its excavator was the possibility that this site could have formed some sort of forward observation post for the Stanegate, similar to that at Birdoswald. If this interpretation is correct, Carrawburgh is visible from Grindon Hill, but Newbrough would have been much the nearest fort and Torney's Fell is well placed to link the two.

It should be stressed once again that this exercise has been purely speculative and there is little evidence that any of these sites actually existed. But it is still interesting to see the postulated new forts and tower plotted on a map with their Wall intervisibilities (**29**) because they fit perfectly into the signalling system already described. They thus continue it for at least another four miles, to the point where the study sector ended at MC 30. Once again every Wall installation can see a Stanegate site and they do so in a pattern that gives each Stanegate installation responsibility for a fairly clearly defined length of Wall.

East of Newbrough the course of the Stanegate road itself is only poorly understood, so that the credible limit of this method of site prospecting has been reached. A few more sites might be suggested, however. For example, although the fort at Washing Well has poor visibility, the bluff line just to its north commands a breathtaking view over the Wall line and from it a single tower could have linked the fort with every Wall installation from Rudchesters to Wallsend. A number of the known and suspected Stanegate sites in the far west also have excellent views of the Wall line and, although no detailed study has yet been performed, the existence of an identical system to that of the study sector is a strong possibility.

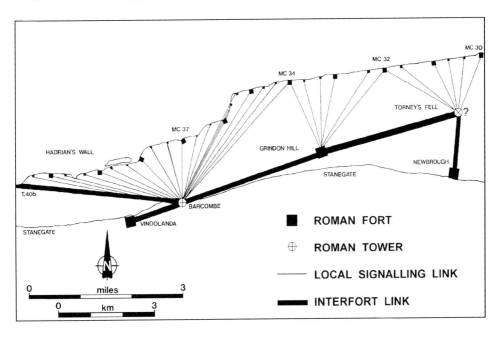

*29 A putative signalling system for Newbrough and Grindon Hill*

*30 Housesteads Wall fort.* Photo G.D.B. Jones

## The signalling system: Wall fort phase

So far the present work has concerned itself only with the very earliest phase of the Wall's development but as this was only very short-lived and was probably never fully completed (Crow 1991), we have probably been studying an intention rather than an operational reality. For, just as the Wall was nearing completion, the frontier was subjected to a major redesign in which a new series of forts, on the line of the Wall itself, were slotted in to replace the older bases on the Stanegate. The abandonment of the forts around which it had been designed would obviously have forced a complete change of orientation on the Wall's signalling system towards bases which its designers could not have foreseen. It is therefore interesting to attempt to see how the Romans coped with this problem, always assuming that, with the greater proximity of the main frontier forces, they attempted to do so at all.

Of course, to some extent, the Stanegate was never abandoned. As already stated, Carvoran remained in use or was quickly reoccupied, as did Vindolanda, Pike Hill and T 45a and we can now tentatively add Castlesteads and perhaps T 40b to this list. In some areas, therefore, the disruption can be exaggerated. Nevertheless, elsewhere the old installations did completely cease to exist. The discontinuity is nowhere more apparent than at Birdoswald where, on a two mile front, even the course of the Wall was moved, onto a more northerly line which, although in full view of the new fort (the original line would not have been), was completely out of sight of the Stanegate.

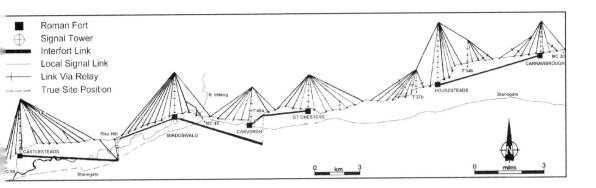

*31 The signalling system of Hadrian's Wall: Wall fort phase*

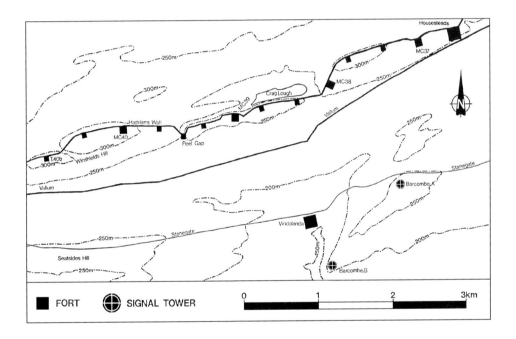

*32 Map of Vindolanda and its environs*

In fact the Romans seem to have done remarkably well. The new forts would appear to have been deliberately sited in highly visible positions since, unlike the Stanegate forts, they were frequently built on hilltops, and it is possible to map out a signalling system with the Wall forts in place (**31**). Even so, a number of sites now required relaying via a second Wall installation before their signals could reach a fort or strategic tower (e.g. MC 33, T 41a and T 54a). One, MC 48, would have required a double relay via T 48a and T 48b before its signals could reach the fort of Birdoswald, despite the relative proximity of the two sites.

*33 Vindolanda from Barcombe B*

Yet, whilst showing the obvious characteristics of a 'botch job', the local signalling system of the restyled frontier was a considerable achievement, especially in view of the inflexibility of the raw material. The long range, inter-fort system also remained largely secure. Castlesteads is linked to Birdoswald via the old Pike Hill tower. Birdoswald communicates with Carvoran via T 45a, which also serves to link Carvoran with Great Chesters, and Housesteads and Carrawburgh are actually intervisible. But in one area the modified system does appear to break down.

In the initial design, the area around Vindolanda had been one of the most neatly laid out parts of the system (**32**). Under the new regime, however, it initially appeared to become unworkable. By assuming that all of the milecastles and turrets between MC 38 and T 40a were relayed into Housesteads via T 37b, it is just about possible to devise local links between every Wall installation on the sector and the forts of Housesteads and Great Chesters (**31**). But the forts themselves are not intervisible and, until recently, there was no known installation that could have served as a relay station between them. We were therefore faced with a break in the inter-fort chain without which Hadrian's Wall could cease to be a single unified system under emergency conditions. Worse still, neither fort can see Vindolanda, which now appears to have been in use throughout the period, but with its signal tower on Barcombe abandoned (Woodfield 1966).

Fortunately, a solution can now be offered in the form of a second tower, Barcombe B[2] on the westernmost spur of Barcombe Hill, almost due south of Vindolanda. At ground level, the site's principle view is to the south and west and its view to the north-east, towards Housesteads, is limited. But despite its apparently awkward position tucked into

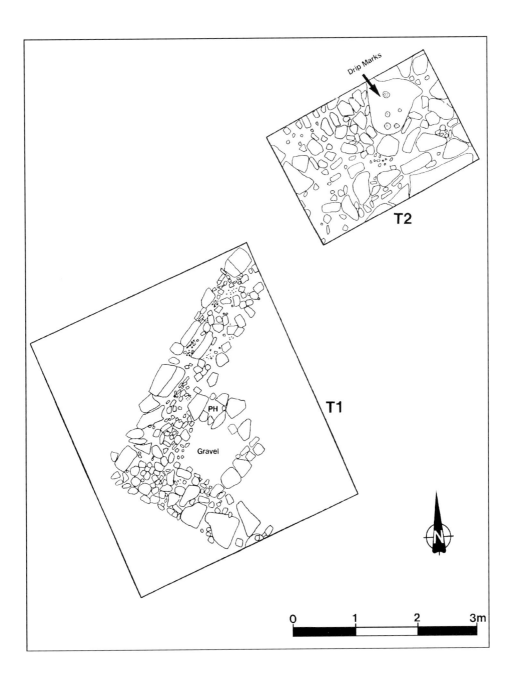

*34  Barcombe B, excavation plan*

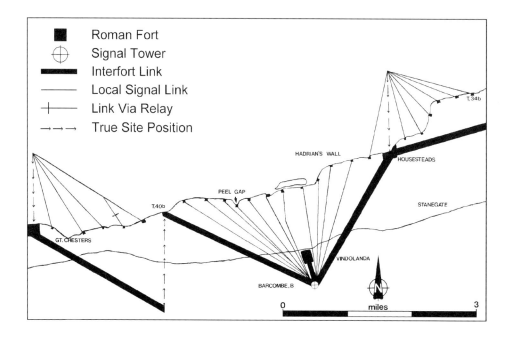

*35 The signalling system around Barcombe B*

the side of Barcombe, a tower on this site would, from full height, have been able to see Housesteads, although it could not have seen a single yard further. The site would also have been intervisible with T 40b, which could have linked it Great Chesters. Moreover, it could see all of the Wall installations between T 40b and Housesteads, including the recently discovered secondary tower in Peel Gap (Crow 1987), which lay out of sight of the original Barcombe tower, and it has a magnificent view of Vindolanda (**33**). Small-scale excavations by the writer have uncovered what appears to be a Roman stone tower on the site with walls of exactly the same thickness as those of T 45a (**34**). But as the only datable material recovered was a single sherd of second-century glass, its foundation date is still somewhat open to question. Assuming that it does prove to be Hadrianic, however, the signalling system for the area would become that shown in **35**, and with the addition of this one relay tower the sector is once again neatly and efficiently linked together.

## Notes

1 The dating of Carvoran is insecure but a Trajanic occupation is suggested by a Domitianic official corn measure found on the site on which Domitian's name had been erased after his fall.
2 I am grateful to Mr R.E. Birley for bringing this site to my attention.

# 3 Hadrian's Wall peripheral systems

## The outpost forts

The layout of the Tyne-Solway frontier, at all stages of its development, reflects the strategy underlying Roman *Limes* systems. It was, in essence, a compromise dictated by the frontier defences' need to fulfil two broad operational requirements, which demanded mutually exclusive patterns of troop deployment. The frontier army had, above all, to be able to defend the province against a full-scale invasion. This demanded large concentrations of force set at strategic centres and able, at short notice, to intercept and destroy any external force, or at least hold it until help could be brought from the legions stationed further to the south. But the ever more tightly policed frontiers (Luttwak 1976, ch. 2) developed during the late first and second centuries AD required strict border controls to be enforced to prevent even the smallest raiding party from penetrating Roman soil. In this role large, anti-invasion concentrations were useless, for all their undoubted power, as they were far too easy to side step for small, highly mobile bands, and a different approach was needed. Total control of an entire frontier line requires a dispersal of forces along the border to permit intensive patrolling, observation, customs cover and the scrutiny of persons wishing to cross. But such a diffuse deployment is extremely vulnerable in the event of a major attack. This is because, although the frontier's total garrison might be large, its dispersal means that no single point will have the manpower necessary to withstand concentrated enemy forces, even though these may be numerically far weaker than the total strength of the defending army. Worse still, once penetrated, such a shallow, linear system is left with its communications disrupted, making any subsequent concentration of, and concerted action by, the surviving frontier forces more difficult.

The course taken by the Romans seems to have been to seek a balance between the two requirements. Under the Stanegate system their forces were indeed dispersed, but instead of being spread out evenly, they remained in relatively large, whole unit groupings. This formula, in conjunction with patrolling and observation from a small number of more minor installations, would have allowed for reasonably tight border control. But, in the event of a major threat, the individual units could still have been fairly rapidly recombined to form a single substantial force. Defences to intermediate level threats were also quickly to hand as the individual units were large enough to withstand a considerable assault by themselves and, if necessary, they could rapidly combine with their immediate neighbours. Nevertheless, as the Stanegate was still a very open frontier, it could not have guaranteed the degree of preclusiveness that appears to have been demanded by the second-century Empire. In other words, it could not have provided the certainty that any threat to the province, however small, would be dealt with on or before the frontier line. The need to avoid all but a minimum of further dispersal, so as to retain the major groupings intact, was met by the construction of Hadrian's Wall, which is probably best seen as a labour-saving device to allow the tightest possible frontier control with the least possible manpower.

The success of this otherwise flexible compromise would naturally have been heavily dependent on intelligence gathering. Under normal circumstances the Roman army enjoyed considerable advantages over its barbarian adversaries, which allowed it to face numerically stronger forces with confidence. As well as its superiority in tactics, training, equipment, discipline and logistics, it had another advantage that has received surprisingly little attention and that is the very fact of its being a permanent, professional, standing force. This gave it a great deal more than just cohesiveness and *esprit de corps*. It also meant that from the moment an outside people decided on confrontation, time was on the Romans' side. For, although the Romans needed time to concentrate their frontier units, these were, at least, already in being, whilst, except for a small elite around the chieftain (Tacitus, *Germania*, 13-15), the barbarians usually had to raise their army from nothing by means of a tribal levy of some sort. Assuming that their intelligence was functioning properly, the Romans should thus have been in a position to launch pre-emptive strikes and stamp out potential danger before the enemy had even had time to raise their army fully.

If, however, Roman intelligence failed to detect signs of unrest, or omitted, for some reason, to warn the frontier forces, the dangers inherent in what was still a relatively diffuse troop deployment could be catastrophic. For the provincial army might then be caught with its component units dispersed, and swept aside. Something of exactly this nature seems to have happened during the so-called 'Great Barbarian Conspiracy' of AD 367. On this occasion Roman control of the province could not be fully restored until a relief force of field army units was sent over from the Continent, under the command of Count Theodosius.

The fourth-century historian Ammianus Marcellinus tells us that after the final recovery of Britain Theodosius disbanded a Roman force called the *Areani* (Ammianus Marcellinus, 28-3-8), whose role had been 'to scurry about hither and thither over long distances to keep our commanders informed of the commotions amongst neighbouring peoples'. On the promise of booty this force had betrayed the Roman army which had thus been caught unawares. The *Areani* were, then, at least a part of a regular intelligence gathering service and they can probably be identified, if only by function, with the units of *exploratores* (scouts) recorded in military inscriptions from earlier times.

The intelligence screen for Hadrian's Wall was presumably based in the outpost forts, of which there were generally five: Birrens, Netherby and Bewcastle in the west (**36**), and Risingham and High Rochester in the east (**37**). These were large, and obviously important, forts. In Hadrianic times, they may only have held *quingenary* (500-strong) cohorts, but each of the three western forts rapidly acquired a larger *Cohors Milliaria Equitata* (RIB 968, 988 & 2094). With 1040 men, 240 of which were cavalry (Holder 1980, 7 and 1982, 37), these were the largest auxiliary units in the Roman army. Their mixture of mounted troops and infantry made them the ideal units to conduct long-range reconnaissance, as well as making them substantial and balanced combat teams capable of

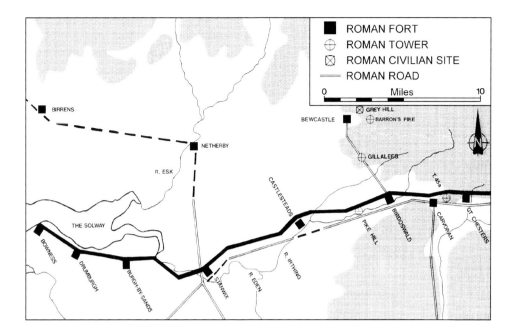

*36 Hadrian's Wall's western outposts*

holding off all but a really major attack. More clandestine intelligence work may have been the role of the *exploratores* and there is considerable evidence for these units at the outpost forts. Both Risingham and High Rochester are known to have held a *Numerus Exploratorum* (RIB 1235 & 1262) alongside their main garrisons, which were again milliary cohorts, and at Netherby the very name of the fort was Castra Exploratorum, or fort of the scouts (Rivet & Smith 1979, 302).

Given the function of these outposts, it must have been imperative for them to have signalling links back to Hadrian's Wall. Recent work seems to have discovered a link between Bewcastle and its nearest Wall fort, Birdoswald, which lies some six and a quarter miles to the south. Birdoswald is linked to Bewcastle by a Roman road known as the Maiden Way and a signal tower has long been known to exist beside this road, four and a half miles to the north of Birdoswald, on a hill called Gillalees Beacon. Unfortunately, although the tower, which is usually called Robin Hood's Butt, has a magnificent view to the south, taking in almost the whole of Hadrian's Wall from Housesteads to Carlisle, it is unable to see Bewcastle because of the shape of Gillalees Beacon itself and the tower's position on it.

Gillalees is a commanding hill which dominates the country for miles around, especially to its south, west and north-west. It is steep-sided, particularly on its north and west faces, but has a broad flat top. Bewcastle is tucked into the bottom of the hill's north face, beside the Kirk Beck and is only visible from the very northern edge of the summit (**38**). The signal tower, on the other hand, lies just below the summit at the top of the south face and although, from its tower top, this installation would have been able to see

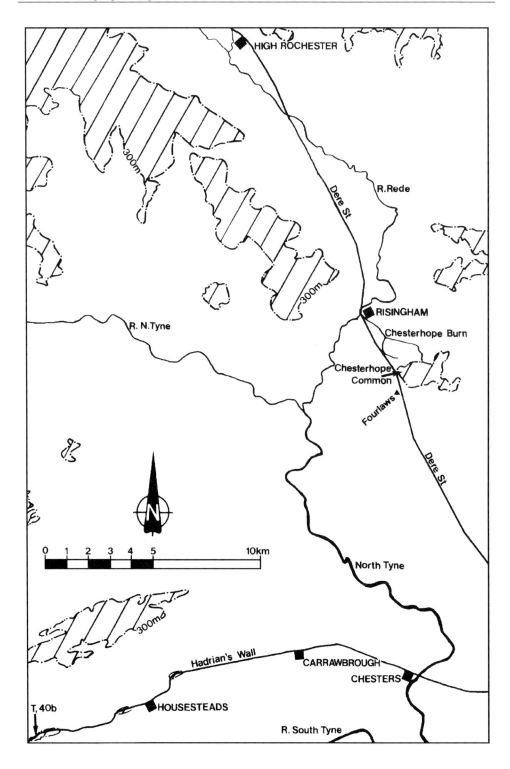

37 *Hadrian's Wall's eastern outpost forts*

*38  Bewcastle fort (under castle and hamlet) from Gillalees Beacon north side*

the entire hilltop, the drop down to Bewcastle is such that the fort remains out of sight. To explain this curious state of affairs, Richmond (1933, 241) suggested that the tower was deliberately sited so that its signals would be invisible to the north. Thus, on detecting danger, Bewcastle could send a rider up Gillalees to the tower, which could then signal back to the Wall and co-ordinate the laying of ambushes without the enemy being aware that they had been detected. Even if the Romans had wanted to conceal their signals, however, rather than exploit the deterrent value of their very visibility, it seems questionable whether Roman signalling methods could, over this long link, have conveyed the sort of high grade information and instructions needed to co-ordinate ambushes. Further, this model rests on two mistaken assumptions. Firstly, that by re-siting the tower the Romans could have made it visible from both Birdoswald and Bewcastle and, secondly, that because the tower is invisible from Bewcastle it is invisible from the north as a whole. In fact, when standing to its full height, the tower would have been visible for many miles to its north. Yet the flat topped, steep sided nature of Gillalees Beacon means that there is nowhere on it from which both forts could have been viewed simultaneously, even from the top of a Roman tower. It thus appeared more likely that Robin Hood's Butt was only half of a signalling chain made up of not one, but two towers and an attempt was, therefore, made to find its twin.

The obvious solution would have been a second tower on the north side of the same hill, but searches by both the author and earlier workers have produced no trace and an alternative site had to be sought. There are, in fact, only three places visible from both Bewcastle and the full height of the Gillalees tower. These are Barron's Pike, at the east

*39 Barron's Pike tower*

end of the Kirk Beck valley, Black Preston, a hill about a mile further north, and Grey Hill, which makes up the north side of the Kirk Beck valley and faces Gillalees. Black Preston held nothing that could be detected by field walking, while Grey Hill has only a Romano-British structure, excavated by the writer and thought to be agricultural (Woolliscroft, Nevell & Swain 1989). Barron's Pike, however, has long been known to carry an archaeological monument classed as a ring cairn. Almost simultaneous re-examinations by both Topping (1987) and the author (Woolliscroft 1988) cast doubts on this interpretation, however, and reclassified the feature as a Roman tower. The site consists of a ring ditch 26m across and surrounded by the very fragmentary remains of an upcast mound. This ditch encloses an area 18m in diameter, the central area of which, although obscured by a survey cairn, appears to form a raised platform of approximately rectangular shape (**39**). The ditch on the well-preserved and apparently rock-cut west side is just over 3m wide and has the 'V'-shaped profile (**40**) typical of Roman military sites (Woolliscroft 1990). The interior is reached by means of a single entrance causeway 1.3m wide that again shows typically Roman, concave ditch butt ends. This basic layout is so typical of free-standing Roman watchtowers that although excavation would obviously be desirable, the site's identity now appears reasonably secure and Barron's Pike all but guaranteed to be the second Bewcastle-Birdoswald signal tower.

Barron's Pike's field of view would appear to offer further confirmation of its nature, for as well as enjoying a splendid view of Bewcastle and being directly intervisible with Carvoran on both the Stanegate and Hadrian's Wall, it offers an explanation for the apparently illogical siting of Robin Hood's Butt. The Butt is at virtually the last point south still able to see it, suggesting that the Gillalees tower's odd position was simply an

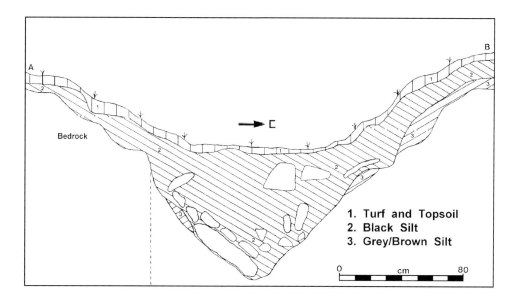

*40 Barron's Pike: ditch section*

attempt to reduce the range of the long link back to Bewcastle to the minimum possible. The possibilities do not end there, however, for Barron's Pike is a quite remarkable lookout site. Situated as it is at the apex of the Solway basin, at an altitude of over 1000ft (355m), it commands a magnificent view stretching from the Lake District to the southern uplands of Scotland and taking in the whole of the line of Hadrian's Wall from Carlisle to the sea. Furthermore, the ring of low hills overlooking the next outpost fort at Netherby is plainly visible, as are the hills around Birrens, especially the prominent, flat-topped ridge of Burnswark, the site of a Roman fortlet.

The outposts tend to be pictured as isolated stations set outside Roman territory, surrounded by and imposed upon a potentially hostile local population. But there is evidence that the territory of the Brigantes, and thus probably of Rome, stretched some way north of Hadrian's Wall in the west. There is, for example, an inscription dedicated to the goddess Brigantia from Birrens (RIB 2091), although this could simply indicate the presence of a soldier of Brigantian origin and imply nothing about the find spot. More interesting, however, is an inscription from Italy recording the career of a high equestrian official whose name is lost. Amongst a series of positions, culminating in the Prefecture of Egypt, he held an office referred to as *Censitori Brittonum Anavionensium* (CIL, 40, Pt 2, 5213), probably under Trajan. Anava seems to be the River Annan, again in the region of Birrens (Rivet & Smith 1979, 249), and it is unlikely that a 'Censor of the Britons' would be operating in this area unless it was part of the Empire. The Solway basin is very much a geographical unit and even the Solway itself presents less of a barrier than might be thought because it is fordable.[1] It is therefore conceivable that, whilst Hadrian's Wall took the shortest and tactically soundest route to the sea, the true political boundary lay further north. This would mean that the western outpost forts, instead of being embattled enclaves in barbarian territory, would have been the true frontier forts and would probably have been sited on Roman soil. The writer's own discovery of Romano-British civil occupation on Grey hill, overlooking Bewcastle (Woolliscroft, Nevell & Swain 1989) from a range of about 2km, certainly suggests reasonably peaceful conditions (although the building was eventually destroyed by fire at some time after the early fourth century). It might be considered significant that, unlike their eastern counterparts, the western outposts were deployed in an east-west line and not strung out along the main route into Scotland.

A frontier fort, however, has different communication needs to an outpost. The first requirement of an outpost fort is for vertical links back to its own lines and, as well as the road and signal links between Bewcastle and the Wall, Netherby is known to be linked by road to Carlisle and Stanwix. A frontier fort, on the other hand, requires lateral communications along the frontier.

No road is yet known between Bewcastle and Netherby, but Birrens and Netherby were linked by means of a branch of the Netherby to Carlisle road. The tower on Barron's Pike, however, opens up the possibility that there were also lateral signalling links between the outposts. It should be stressed from the start that this has yet to be proved, so we are once again entering the realm of speculation but, as already mentioned, Barron's Pike can see to within about a mile of Netherby. It would have been a simple matter to link the two sites by means of a single tower on one of the hills which overlook the fort. Likewise, a single tower could, in theory, have linked Barron's Pike with Birrens, although the range is probably excessive. More likely is a link between Birrens and Netherby, which again could have been established over a number of routes using just one tower for each fort. All three forts could thus have been linked together as well as being connected back to the Wall, and even a road link between Bewcastle and Netherby may still await discovery. Indeed, there were close parallels to this network in the medieval period when Bewcastle, Netherby and Carlisle all had castles within them and Birrens had Hoddom Castle close by. Gillalees Beacon had the signal beacon after which it was named and there was another beacon on Grey Hill close to Barron's Pike. If the political boundary of the Roman Empire did then extend north of the Wall in the western sector it would mean that, should these potential lateral links be proven, Birrens, Netherby and Bewcastle, far from being remote and dangerous outstations, could have been the central elements of an outer *Limes* of roads and signal/watchtowers guarding the true frontier of the Roman world.

The two eastern outposts are slightly different. For a start, they are set out on a north-south line along Dere Street, the main Roman road into Scotland (*see* **37**), and not on an east-west axis parallel to the Wall. They were also not part of the original Hadrianic plan for the area, for both appear to be Antonine foundations (Richmond 1936 & 1940, 101f and Casey & Savage 1980), albeit High Rochester had earlier seen late first-century activity. Their political position, and that of the surrounding country, is uncertain. They were certainly no longer in Brigantia. But as they were probably either in or on the border of the territory of the supposedly philo-Roman Votadini, they have often been assumed to have been providing some form of protection for that tribe (e.g. Frere 1987, 91 & 133ff) as well as for the Wall itself. Exactly what form this protection took, however, and the exact status of the Votadini in Roman eyes, remains distinctly uncertain, as much of the evidence is circumstantial.

What, if any, signalling arrangements were provided to link the two forts, both to each other and back to Hadrian's Wall, is also uncertain. At one time it was thought that a signalling site existed at Four Laws near Risingham (NY 905830), where, as we saw in chapter one, I.A. Richmond (1940, 101f) discovered a series of seven circular stone standings (*c.*3.3m in diameter and 5.2m apart) which he believed to be a relay station. Unfortunately, although this identification seems to have been widely accepted, the site is very ill equipped to act in such a role. As Richmond admits, it cannot see Risingham (*c.*3km to the north) thanks to a low hilltop separating the two, but contrary to past belief it is also out of sight of Hadrian's Wall. Richmond did claim that the site was visible from Limestone Corner (MC 30), 11km to the south, which should have given it a link back to the Wall forts of Chesters and Carrawburgh, but he was mistaken. Four Laws cannot, in fact, see any point on the Wall line and he was, almost certainly, fooled (as was the author very briefly) by a rocky outcrop called Butterland Fell, only 3-4km south of the site, which does, from a distance, look very like Limestone Corner, even through binoculars. Furthermore, the standings are ranged from north to south along Dere street rather than east to west as we might expect of a system designed for north-south signalling. As they encroach upon the line of the Roman road, it should have always been apparent that the two were not contemporary. Fortunately recent excavations have now settled the issue (Binns 1961) by showing that the structures are relatively modern platforms built so long after the road had gone out of use that 10-15cm of soil had had time to form on its surface.

There is, however, one place from which the entire system could have been linked together by a single tower: a hilltop called Chesterhope Common (NY 9183/4), only *c.*800m to the north-east of Four Laws. This site has a quite remarkable field of view, exceeding even that of Barron's Pike. To its south it can see a section of Hadrian's Wall stretching from T 31b to T 40b which includes a direct view of Housesteads fort and possibly Carrawburgh (although ironically not Limestone Corner) and, to its north, it can see not only Risingham, but High Rochester as well. It cannot, however, see back along Dere street to Halton Chesters, its nearest Wall fort, and at least two more relay towers would have been needed to link these two. Unfortunately, at the time of writing, most of the hilltop is covered by an impenetrable unthinned pine plantation and the author has been physically unable to make anything more than the most cursory search for surface signs of a site. But there is a certain amount of, albeit tenuous, evidence that such a tower may have existed. Risingham and High Rochester are both located in the only possible places in their vicinities from which they could have carried out their wider duties whilst still being able to see it; in the case of High Rochester, this has led to a rather unconventional fort position. As Selkirk (1983, 73 & 98) has pointed out, Roman forts do not seek out high defensible places like medieval castles. Instead, they tend to be situated on fairly low-lying ground, often on small plateaux, close to water, and when forts are strung out along roads they often occur where the road crosses a river. There are, however, obvious exceptions to this rule, notably the Wall forts of Hadrian's Wall and the later Antonine Wall, which tend to be sited on conspicuous hilltops. As we saw in chapter 2, this may be a sign that forts were being sited to improve their signalling position. All of the outpost forts except High Rochester conform to this trend, with Risingham standing close to the River Rede, Netherby on the Esk, and Birrens and Bewcastle on low plateaux close to streams. High Rochester could also have been built on such a site, as there is an ideal Roman fort position *c*.500m to its west, at NY 827984, where the confluence of the Sills Burn and the Rede has created the plateau now occupied by the Redesdale army camp. Instead, the fort sits on high ground overlooking this position, with an improved field of view, but on a much more exposed site which is also much further from water. The improved view to the north which this hilltop gives the fort would, no doubt, have been an advantage. But the availability of similar views was not enough to tempt the other outposts onto higher ground. Instead, they may all have followed Bewcastle in posting watchtowers on nearby high ground to extend their observation cover. High Rochester's position does, however, allow it to see Chesterhope Common from tower top height and, although, again, a relay tower could have been used instead, this fact may have had some influence on its siting. Risingham is in a much more conventional position down in the Rede valley, but it does stand *c*.200m to the east, and on the opposite side, of the Chesterhope Burn from the line of the (much older) Roman road. This may not be particularly surprising, for the fort's position is an excellent building platform and the Burn is only a brook. Nevertheless, it may also be relevant that the fort is situated on the one usable spot with an excellent view south along the Burn's very narrow valley, up which, unlike anywhere else in the vicinity, it is intervisible with the potential tower site on Chesterhope Common.

The writer freely admits that all this could be purely coincidence and that nothing of substance can be built on such flimsy evidence. But it will be interesting to see what emerges when the timber on Chesterhope Common is harvested and one of the best potential signalling positions anywhere on the Hadrian's Wall system becomes available for study.

## The Cumberland coast defences

Hadrian's Wall proper may end at Bowness on Solway but, with the Scottish coast still only a short boat trip away, its western flank was protected by a series of shore defences which reach at least as far south as Maryport (**41**) and possibly further. In essence, the Wall itself and these coastal defences are merely two different parts of the same system. They show so many design similarities that the coastal system becomes little more than a continuation of the Wall's basic framework, whilst omitting the curtain wall itself, and so one might expect their signalling arrangements to be identical. The two share the same regular installation pattern, since the coastal mile-fortlets and towers correspond exactly to the milecastles and turrets on the Wall line. Both have a series of forts, set at similar intervals and in similarly prominent positions. There have even been claims that the coastal works had a running barrier to stand in lieu of Hadrian's Wall, in the form of ditches on the Cardurnock Peninsula in the north, and a pair of parallel timber fences or palisades further south, around Silloth (Jones 1976 and Higham & Jones 1985, 30ff). Excavations by the writer have now discredited the Silloth palisade (Woolliscroft & Jones, forthcoming), and a number of doubts have been expressed over the northern ditches (Bellhouse 1981, and 1989, 5ff). Yet the system is linked by a lateral road and the prospect

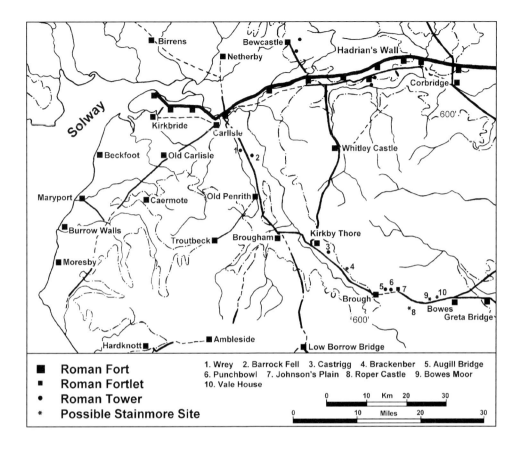

*41 Roman military sites in northern England.* After Farrar

of some sort of running barrier can not be wholly ruled out. Nevertheless, there are a number of differences in the design of the coastal sector which do appear likely to alter its signalling arrangements somewhat; significant gaps in our knowledge also make the sector more difficult to study.

For example, unlike Hadrian's Wall, the coastal defences were built on a truly rigid spacing system, with the sites almost always set at exact one third of a Roman mile intervals (Bellhouse 1989). This means that this part of the line did not use the subtle spacing shifts that we have seen employed on the Wall itself to facilitate signalling. There are signs, however, of a slightly different approach for, in a number of areas, the course of the line itself seems to have been chosen with signalling in mind. For example, in some sectors, such as the stretch between Tower 3b and Milefortlet 5 (*see* **44**), the frontier sites are set significantly further back from the shore line than is usual and hence do not enjoy anything like the best possible view over the sea. At first sight this seems irrational, especially as coastal erosion here means that they would have been even further from the water in Roman times. Yet had these sites been any closer to the sea, they would not have been able to signal to the fort of Bowness. Thus the entire line has been brought inland, despite the consequent loss of superior observation positions. On other occasions distinct kinks have been formed in the line and these may also have been partly intended to facilitate signalling as they allow particular sites to occupy advantageous positions without upsetting the spacing regime. For example, MF 2 would appear to have lain at the end of a low spit of land which once jutted out into the Solway, but has now largely eroded away (Bellhouse 1969, 69ff & fig. 3). Such a position would, no doubt, have improved its view over the water and thus its lookout capacity. But it would also have enabled the fortlet to see every other coastal site on the Cardurnock peninsula, including the fort of Bowness. As many of the other minor installations in its vicinity are not intervisible with the fort, the milefortlet could have served as a key relay site.

Signalling on the system would also have been helped by the fact that most of the coastal forts are sited in highly visible positions, and Beckfoot and Maryport in particular can be seen for miles up and down the line. Maryport and, to a lesser extent Bowness, also form what might be called visual watersheds because, although they can see considerable lengths of the system to both sides, they stand on ground that almost none of the sites to their north and south can see beyond.

Despite such signs of thoughtful design, however, the rigidity of the system has been allowed to produce the occasional eccentricity and this is nowhere more apparent than on Swarthy Hill (NY 067397). This hill dominates the coastline in its vicinity and is one of the best observation positions on the entire line, for although it is very close to the shore it stands 31m above the waves. Yet the spacing system decreed that the summit should remain unoccupied. No allowance was made for its special position and instead of occupying the highest point TR 20b was built halfway up the hill's northern flank, whilst MF 21 lies some way beneath the summit on the southern side. As a result, the two installations cannot see each other, and neither is in the best observation position. Furthermore, although both sites can see the fort of Maryport, TR 20b can only do so from the full height of a 10m tower and had it been just 1m lower, it would have had to signal back to MF 20 to get its signals relayed to the fort.

The second problem in studying the coast is that, unlike Hadrian's Wall, we have yet to determine the full extent of the system. In other words, we simply do not know, as yet, where it ends. The traditional assumption has been that the line would continue as far as St Bee's Head, where the English coast turns sharply away from Scotland (E. Birley 1961, 128), but there is little evidence to support this. The most southerly minor installation discovered to date is TR 26b, to the south of Maryport, although, as the system seems unlikely to have ended with a tower, we might expect at least one more fortlet (MF 27) to lie under the modern village of Flimby. This is only two-thirds of the way to St Bee's Head, however. Yet searches from the air and on the ground by R.L. Bellhouse, the discoverer of so much of the line, have failed to find any trace of sites further south and Bellhouse (1981) himself has reached the conclusion that the tower and milefortlet chain may well have stopped at this point. This would explain a conspicuous change in the way that the forts are positioned further south. For although a fort chain does continue on down the coast, there is a switch away from the exposed but conspicuous positions mentioned above, to more sheltered sites hidden away in the bays. This change cannot be explained by a lack of suitable terrain and must thus have been deliberate, because the forts

*42 Maryport fort.* Photo G.D.B. Jones

of Burrow Walls and Moresby both have promontories immediately to their north which are just as conspicuous as the one on which Maryport stands. Indeed, had Burrow Walls stood on its promontory it would have been intervisible with Maryport. It is true that these high points could have been occupied by relay towers so that the forts could have remained in contact with any surrounding towers and milefortlets, whilst themselves enjoying more shelter, but even this would contrast suspiciously with the pattern further north. Besides, no such relays have ever been found and the situation, as we have it, would only seem to make sense if the forts no longer had to communicate with minor installations strung out along the foreshore.

There is, however, one possible hint that the system may have continued much further, or at least that it might have resumed further south after a break. T.W. Potter's excavations at Ravenglass located a ditch under the late Hadrianic coastal fort, which he took to belong to an installation of the milefortlet type (Potter 1979, 14ff). He also points to a second coastal site, about one Roman mile to the south, as a putative second fortlet and suggests that the system may have rounded St Bee's Head and continued on south. The second fortlet has now been fairly convincingly discredited by Bellhouse (1989, 61ff), but the same writer's attempts to dismiss the Ravenglass site, whilst sufficient to give pause for thought, are not so conclusive. Dr Potter would argue that a Ravenglass fortlet cannot have stood alone and, whilst this is not necessarily the case, it is still tempting to wonder whether the system did get this far and, if so, how much further.

Such a lengthy system would have faced major practical problems. For example, the next known coastal fort to the south of Ravenglass is Lancaster, at least 40 miles away by the shoreline. This means that as the Ravenglass fortlet would already be MF 55 or 56, a system continuing one fort further would actually be longer than Hadrian's Wall itself. Moreover, even more distant destinations might come to be considered now that coastal towers of second-century appearance have been found on Anglesey. Such massive systems would have required phenomenal manpower, especially if they retained the same three sites per mile spacing density. Yet, south of Ravenglass, it is difficult to see where this could have come from as there are simply not enough coastal forts to provide it. It is also rather difficult to see what purpose such lengthy defences would have served or how they might have operated. There is obviously little point in a coastal watch system unless, having detected trouble, it is in a position to do something about it. The garrisons of lightly held towers and fortlets could not ensure security by themselves. This required the presence of garrison centres on the system, for which the minor installations would merely have been eyes and ears. Forts would thus have been the keystones of any effective defence. To function properly they would have needed both to be in communication with the line installations, so that these could summon their help, and frequent enough to ensure that such help would arrive in time. But south of Ravenglass few such forts were available.

It is still, of course, possible that specific vulnerable sections of coast may have been guarded or provided with observation cover and it is obviously feasible that individual coastal forts might have deployed more localised lookout systems on their flanks. But such arrangements need not have been linked, or indeed relevant, to Hadrian's Wall's own coastal defences and, under these circumstances, the present writer is, as yet, unconvinced that these even ran as far as Ravenglass, let alone further. Having said that, it also has to be admitted that neither TR 26b nor Flimby seem particularly logical places to end the system. Bellhouse (1981) has suggested that the reason this spot may have been chosen was a change in the nature of the shoreline here from sandy beaches, on which raiders could land without difficulty, to dangerous rocky cliffs. This sounds eminently plausible and might also explain why the forts further south moved into the bays, since these are the only possible landing places. But it cannot be the whole story. For a start, the beaches do not end at Flimby. Sand beaches continue for another 5km to Workington, and even beyond that are 4-5km of shingle beach on which landings could be made. The cliffs only begin to the south of Harrington (NX 986245), although once they do it is certainly not possible to come ashore safely except at a few clearly identifiable points. Furthermore, the cliff line only extends around St Bee's Head itself and sandy beaches begin again further south. They then run for tens of miles down the coast, extending well beyond Ravenglass, which may have encouraged that fort to maintain its own, possibly separate, lookout system. A more sensible place to have ended the system might thus have been the start of the cliff sector and, interestingly, the late Prof. G.D.B. Jones photographed a site from the air, just to the south of Harrington (NX 98952425), which does at least resemble a fortlet (1982, 296 and pers. comm.). Sadly, Prof. Jones died leaving the site still unexcavated, but if it does prove to be part of the line, it could even be the terminal fortlet.

Obviously, judgement must now be suspended pending further investigation, but there is already one possible counter argument to the system reaching this far: this is the position of the known Roman fort in Workington, Burrow Walls. The situation here could, as already mentioned, have been identical to that at Maryport with the fort standing well above a navigable river mouth, in a position to overlook and exchange signals with shore installations up and down the coast. Yet Burrow Walls lies on low ground close to the water, where it has been partly eroded by the sea. Here there would have been little opportunity to signal to anything and, in view of what we have seen of fort positioning further north, this may be an indication that there was nothing to signal to. The known fort has only produced fourth-century dating material (Bellhouse 1955) and it is not, of course, impossible that it had a Hadrianic predecessor on a radically different site. Such a shift in position would be unprecedented in the area, however, where fort sites, once established, seem to have been retained for centuries with an almost obsessive conservatism and certainly no evidence for such a predecessor has emerged to date.

If the system did then after all end near Flimby there might be a certain logic behind it. For example, TR 26b stands on the furthest point south to be intervisible with Maryport, apart from the high ground to the north of Burrow Walls. The tower itself has a panoramic view over the beaches to its south and, whilst this would have allowed it to link any additional installations to the fort, it could also have kept a reasonable watch by itself. Another point that may be relevant here is the sector's much increased range from the Scottish coast, although the exact significance of this requires that we ask ourselves what sort of threats the coastal defences were set up to defend against and how they were expected to do it.

Bellhouse has repeatedly cautioned scholars against giving undue attention to the coastal sites' mutual intervisibilities or views along the shore and, up to a point, he is right. The sites are obviously not designed to watch each other and their rigid spacing means that the details of their fields of view are often largely fortuitous. Likewise, just as on Hadrian's Wall, there was little point in the minor sites signalling to one another, even though they would still have needed to communicate with the forts. Nevertheless, the very fact that the system was continued on the Hadrian's Wall site spacing pattern suggests that the shore installations were not just concerned with watching the sea. This could have been achieved far more economically by means of isolated observation posts on headlands (as on the late fourth-century Yorkshire coast) or by sites on the higher ground a little inland. The very fact that the densely spaced Cumberland coast system stays so close to the shoreline, often barely above sea level, would suggest that the defences were also watching the foreshore to detect any illicit landings. This was a job that more isolated stations could not have carried out so effectively because, as on the Stanegate, it would still have been relatively easy for small raiding parties to slip past them at night or in misty weather.

The further south the system gets from Bowness, however, the further it gets from potentially hostile coastlines. Scotland is still plainly visible from Flimby, at a range of *c.*40km (25 miles), but this is already much further than Bowness where the distance is barely more than 2km. Increasing distance does not always lessen the risk of attack by seaborne raiders, as the victims of Saxons, Vikings and other marauders have frequently found to their cost. But it would, at least, make it more likely that the raiders would be forced to make part of their sea crossing by day and, on the relatively enclosed waters off Cumbria this would have given the defences a major advantage. We do not yet know whether the Romans maintained a naval presence in Cumbria, although we might expect them to have had some means of taking to the water. But, even if they did not, any raider sailing during the day should have been detected at sea which would have made him more easy to intercept as he landed, even if he did so in darkness. It seems probable, therefore, that raiding parties would try to avoid being out on the water in daylight, at least on the outbound voyage, unless they were in real force. This would in turn mean that they would want to sail in, acquire booty and get off again in the space of a single night. Under darkness, the shore defences would only have been able to detect them at close range, when they had already virtually landed and the closely spaced coastal works appear to be designed to counter just such a threat. But the limitation of this *modus operandi* would be that the raiders could only operate over comparatively short ranges and by the time one gets as far south as Burrow Walls it is likely that such a wholly nocturnal approach would no longer be possible. If so, then the rest of the coast could be protected by a much thinner system.

The final difficulty with the Cumberland coast is that we know far less about its development than we do for Hadrian's Wall itself. Despite G.D.B. Jones's work on the western Stanegate (Higham & Jones 1985, 26ff and Jones 1991) and his recent discovery of the tower at Aldoth (NY 136485), behind Beckfoot (pers. comm.), there is still no sign of an early line backing the system in the way that the Stanegate supported the Wall. Likewise, we still do not understand the chronological relationship between the coastal system and its forts, and no attempt has been made to look for line sites underlying the forts as they frequently did on the Wall. Furthermore, despite the fact that Prof. Jones's work at TR 2b and 4b (Jones 1982 & 1993) suggests that the minor sites had quite a lengthy development, we still do not know if the coast was an original part of the Wall's milecastle and turret chain, or a later addition.

Bellhouse (1970) has argued that the southern part of the system, from MF 9 to TR 26b, was laid out with reference to Maryport, which implies that the fort was planned or already built when the minor works were set up. This has led him to suggest that the original system may have been based on Maryport and the Stanegate period fort of Kirkbride (Bellhouse & Richardson 1982), with the rest of the forts being part of the so-called 'fort decision' which led to the Wall forts of Hadrian's Wall and saw Kirkbride being replaced by Bowness on Solway. This still seems plausible, despite the fact that Maryport, unlike Kirkbride, does not now seem to have been the Trajanic foundation he had assumed (Jarrett 1976). For its square shape is so like that of Kirkbride and so unlike the 'playing card' shape of the Hadrian's Wall and other coastal forts that it is more than tempting to see Maryport as pre-dating the rest of the coastal series. Moreover, a second enclosure has now been seen from the air at Beckfoot and, although this could be just a construction camp, the only plan the writer has been able to find (Bellhouse 1989, 39) shows it as square as and of similar size to Kirkbride. It is thus possible that it too might be an earlier fort and, if so, we might have a primary phase based on Maryport, Kirkbride and Beckfoot, and a post 'fort decision' system using Maryport, Beckfoot and Bowness.

Whatever the truth of such theories, it is certainly hard to believe that the coastal system ever stood without forts. Once again, one of the persistent problems with the study of Roman frontiers is in trying to gauge what sort of threats they faced. One assumes that the Cumberland coast was designed to prevent barbarian raiding parties seeking booty in the hinterland and it is tempting to see such raids as being all rather petty. But just how big was a raiding party? The answer is that we simply do not know but we might be able to gain some idea by replying with questions such as 'how big were Saxon or Viking raids?'. Put like that, the answer to the first question becomes 'quite big enough to be dangerous'. Yet the coastal towers and milefortlets are not, in themselves, capable of dealing with anything more than the smallest of threats and we must assume, once again, that their role was merely to detect trouble and not to suppress it. If so, they would have been utterly useless without forts and, as there is little point in an observation post that cannot tell anyone what it observes, signalling links to those forts would be vital.

## The signalling system

In view of the problems outlined above, the present survey will confine itself to the known sectors between Bowness and Flimby. Chronologically, it will also largely confine itself to the finished form of the system, although a brief description will be offered of the Cardurnock area during a hypothetical period in which Kirkbride was occupied and Bowness was not.

During both periods, the signalling system does indeed appear to have been broadly similar to that of Hadrian's Wall, for the bulk of the sites are directly intervisible with a fort, and those that are not can all communicate with a fort via simple, one stage, relays. For example, if we begin in the north (**43**), all of the sites as far as MF 2 originally had a direct line of sight to Bowness, although the view of the sector between MF 1-2 is now blocked by the remains of the Solway railway bridge. If we then assume that Bellhouse (1969) is correct in locating MF 2 on a now largely eroded projection into the Solway, the milefortlet would have been able to see every site on the Cardurnock peninsular and could thus have linked Bowness with everything between TR 2a and MF 5. MF 2 might also explain the, previously mentioned, odd line of the system between TR 3b and MF 5, because had these sites been any closer to the shoreline, they would have dropped out of sight of this relay.

Between MF 9 and 12,[2] on the southern side of Moricambe, the sites are unknown, but everything between MF 12 and 17 can see Beckfoot. MF 9 cannot see the fort, but its signals could have been relayed via MF 12, along with those of the missing intermediate sites and, as MF 9 can also see MF 5, Bowness and Beckfoot could, themselves, have been linked by a four-stage relay via MF 2, 5, 9 and 12. Finally, Maryport can see everything currently known between MF 17 and TR 26b except for the likely position of TR 20a. But this site can be relayed via either of its neighbours and the fort can also be linked to Beckfoot by means of a single-stage relay via MF 17.

On any hypothetical pre-'fort decision' system, the situation south of MF 9 would have been virtually unchanged, especially if there really was already a fort of some kind at Beckfoot. The only major differences would have been on the Cardurnock Peninsular (**44**), where the signalling system would now have been oriented on Kirkbride. Once again, however, everything would have worked perfectly so long as MF 2 was where Bellhouse has predicted. MF 9 can see Kirkbride, as can MF 5, although again the latter

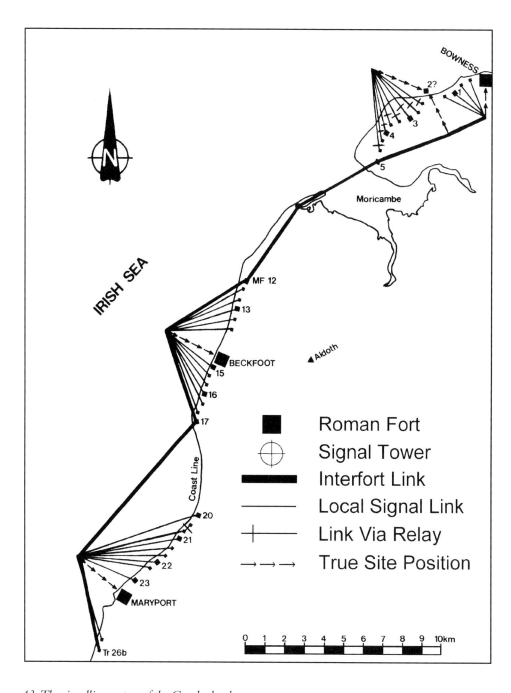

*43 The signalling system of the Cumberland coast*

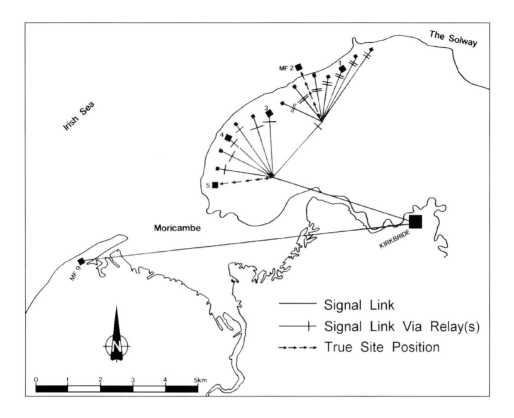

*44 The signalling system of the Cumberland coast, Kirkbride phase*

could not have done so from any nearer the shore. No other site on the peninsula has a direct view to the fort, but MF 5 can see everything from MF 3 to TR 4b and can also see MF 2. MF 2 could thus once more serve as a relay for the remaining sites on the sector, so that every Cardurnock installation could have had signals relayed to Kirkbride, albeit most of the sites between TR 0a and 2b would now require a less efficient two-stage relay.

## The Stainmore

In 1951 Sir Ian Richmond proposed the existence of a long-range Roman signalling system between the fortress of *Legio* VI Victrix at York and the presumed headquarters of Hadrian's Wall at Stanwix, Carlisle. As evidence he cited a series of seven structures (*see* **41**) beside the Roman road over Stainmore (the modern A66) which he took to be five Roman signal towers (Vale House, Bowes Moor, Roper Castle, Brackenber and Barrock Fell) and two fortlets (Castrigg and Maiden Castle (**46**)). This theory has since gained widespread acceptance, although the evidence to support it was and remains very weak. For example, no two of Richmond's sites are of the same design and, at the time, only two (Maiden Castle and Barrock Fell) had been excavated sufficiently to be dated

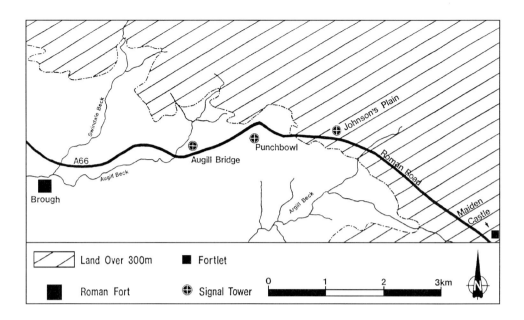

*45 The Stainmore, between Brough and Maiden Castle*

(Collingwood 1915, 1927 & 1931) and these were not contemporary. Richmond's account also contains a certain amount of misinformation. In particular, the supposed tower at Brackenber, which does not in any case resemble a Roman tower, lies in something of a blind hollow which most certainly does not have the skilfully selected field of view that was claimed for it.

Forty years later, things are little better. Bowes Moor is the only additional Richmond site to have been excavated (P. Robinson 1990, 63f), and this is not contemporary with either of the original two. This means that, although again, the system is frequently quoted as fact (e.g. Hartley & Fitts 1988, 37), its existence is still far from proven, and we cannot even be sure that any of the remaining sites are Roman. These problems have also been emphasised by R.A.H. Farrar (1980) and, although his work contains minor errors of its own, especially when he discusses site intervisibilities, it does put the system's validity even further in doubt. Under these circumstances there would seem to be little point in attempting a formal signalling survey. It must be conceded that such a system would have been perfectly feasible, although what use it would have been is unclear, and the writer has spent considerable time seeking new sites (without result) and surveying the best possible route. But, in the absence of stronger evidence for its existence, I do not propose to write what would, almost inevitably, be fiction.

In recent decades, however, aerial surveys by Dr N.J. Higham and Prof. G.D.B. Jones (1985, 44ff) have led to the recognition of an apparently uniform class of monuments on the central Stainmore (**45**), which take a form similar to a normal late first- or early second-century Roman timber watchtower. Three of these sites were found in the 1970s at Augill Bridge (NY 818147), Punchbowl (NY 829148) (**47**) and Johnson's Plain (NY 844149)

*46 Maiden Castle fortlet.* Photo G.D.B. Jones

between Brough and Maiden Castle, and a fourth was recognised earlier by J.K. St Joseph (1951, 53) further west at Castrigg (NY 675222). The sites consist of a circular central mound, surrounded by two penannular ditches, crossed by a single entrance causeway. They are all but identical to the double ditched towers at the southern end of the Gask frontier in Scotland (Woolliscroft & Hoffmann 1997 & 1998 and Glendinning & Dunwell 2000), which appear to date to the AD 80s. Their identity was confirmed by excavations carried out at Augill Bridge soon after its discovery in 1975 (Higham & Jones 1985, 47f) and by the author's own work at Johnson's Plain, in the late 1980s (Woolliscroft & Swain 1991). Both excavations found 'V'-shaped ditches of the usual Roman military type, surrounding towers which show two structural periods (**48**), and were thus presumably fairly long-lived. But as no dating evidence was found at either site, their chronological context remains uncertain.

As for their role, Castrigg stands on the furthest point east to be visible from the fort of Kirkby Thore and would certainly make sense as both a watchtower and a signalling relay, but the eastern group are very different. The known examples occur at *c*.13-1400m intervals between Brough and the fortlet of Maiden Castle. But, as there are currently *c*.3km gaps between the fort and fortlet and each end of the tower line, two more may still await discovery. Indeed, at one point it was thought that a fourth tower had been found at Augill Castle, between Brough and the known site at Augill Bridge (Higham & Jones 1985, 49) but, although this site was subsequently excavated and discredited by the author, this does not rule out the potential for further towers to come to light. Be that as it may,

*47 The Roman tower of Punchbowl, Stainmore*

the known sites seem to form a regular sequence, all of whose members could see all of the others, so that all of the towers enjoy direct communications with both Maiden Castle and Brough, which are themselves intervisible with each other. There would thus seem to be far more towers here than was necessary if their purpose was simply to form part of a long distance signalling chain. Indeed the ideal relay position to carry signals from (or via) Brough to the east would be Maiden Castle itself, so that the entire tower line might appear to be superfluous in this role. It could, of course, be suggested that they may have been built as subsidiary relays to allow the system to function in poor visibility, and this semi-mountainous area is certainly capable of some very unpleasant weather. But it has been the writer's experience that when conditions close in to the extent that Brough can no longer see Maiden Castle, the towers usually lose sight of each other as well. This means that there are too many sites for a fair weather signalling chain, but too few for an all weather one, and the system makes much more sense as a series of watch posts with purely localised duties such as guarding the road.

Nevertheless, the question still remains open and a number of models could be put forward. For example, it may still be possible that the towers were supplementing a long range signalling system by providing observation cover as well as occasional poor weather relay facilities. They may be an attempt to keep a close watch on the strategic Stainmore Pass to protect road communications or, as Carlisle is now known to date to the AD 70s, rather earlier than had been expected (Groves 1990), they may even be part of some form of pre-Agricolan proto-frontier through northern England. Sadly, however, the only current certainty on the Stainmore is that a great deal more work will be needed before

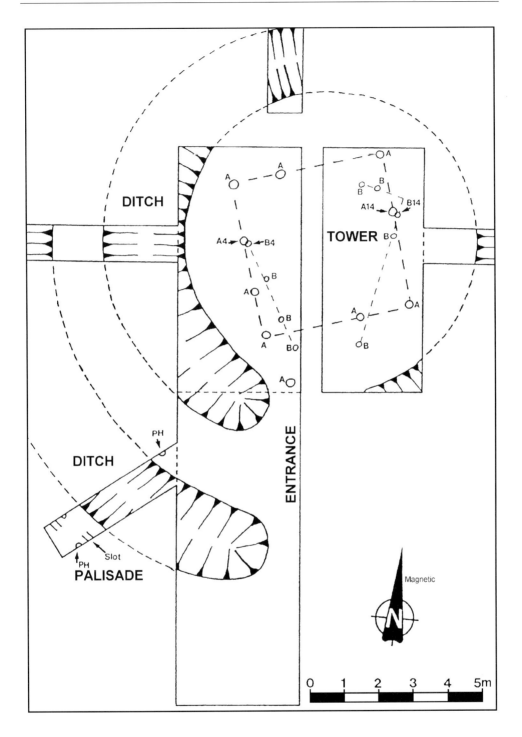

*48 Johnson's Plain tower: plan of central area*

this fascinating area can be properly understood. But, until this has been done, the true nature and purpose of the Roman dispositions must continue to remain uncertain. The present writer would thus not like to press the case for any particular theory, except to stress once again that at present there is no evidence whatever to support an arterial signalling system from the Wall back to York, or indeed any other legionary base.

## Notes

1   Edward I died at Burgh by Sands whilst planning to take an entire army across one of the Solway fords to invade Scotland.
2   Milefortlets 6-8 do not exist. At one time it was thought that Moricambe was dry land in Roman times and Bellhouse originally allowed for a continuation of the system across its mouth. Bellhouse himself (1962) soon exploded this myth, however, by showing that the inlet was much older than had previously been thought. This means that MF 9 should, strictly, be MF 6 and that all of the sites further south have been similarly misnumbered. Nevertheless, the numbering system is still a useful frame of common reference and it is probably too late to alter it now.

# 4 The Wetterau *Limes*

## Aims and choice of study area

As was discussed in the introduction, a study of the signalling arrangements of just one provincial frontier is not enough if we are to look for signs of any underlying unity between different parts of the Roman Empire. Britain was a remote province and the possibility remains that its frontier design approach may not have been applied elsewhere. In order to discount any influence of a 'British army method', therefore, we now need to look at a continental frontier in as great a depth as we have studied Hadrian's Wall. The choice of which frontier to examine was remarkably straightforward. For, once again, as a Roman frontier's signalling system can only be understood by examining the pattern of intervisibilities between its individual installations, a comprehensive signalling study can only be carried out on a frontier where the positions of the great bulk of these installations are already known and available for study. There are, in fact, almost no Roman frontiers outside Britain that have yet been examined in such detail, but one of the very few that has, the German *Limes*, presented an ideal target as it is also the closest and easiest for a British archaeologist to work on.

The *Limes* also has other advantages as a study area. Firstly, it is not confined to a single Roman province, but passes through both Germania Superior and Raetia (**49**). Secondly, it contains within its length, in the Taunus and Wetterau, what appears to be Rome's oldest continental land frontier and, on the Empire-wide scale, second only in age to the Gask system in Scotland. It does, however, have one important weakness for which it is not possible to compensate. The developmental history of the *Limes* is long and extremely complex (Schönberger 1969 & 1985 and Körtüm 1998) and, although its broad outlines are now fairly well established, important points of detail remain unclear especially at the level of the occupational histories of individual sites. A case in point is the story of the *Kleinkastelle*. These small fortlets resemble the milecastles of Hadrian's Wall and may have played a broadly similar role, but there are important differences. For example, unlike the milecastles, the *Kleinkastelle* lie slightly behind the frontier line and are not usually provided with a passage through it. They are also set at longer and much less regular intervals than their British counterparts. Unlike the milecastles, they also do not appear to have been part of the original frontier design and some, at least on the older parts of the line, are built on top of or alongside pre-existing watchtowers. Nor are they all of a uniform design, for whilst the great bulk do indeed resemble milecastles, or, more correctly, Cumberland Coast milefortlets, a significant minority are much bigger and barely belong to the same class of monument. One such example, KK Haselheck (Baatz 1980), near the fort of Echzell in the Wetterau, is as large as 0.4ha (1 acre), which is larger than the Stanegate fortlet of Haltwhistle

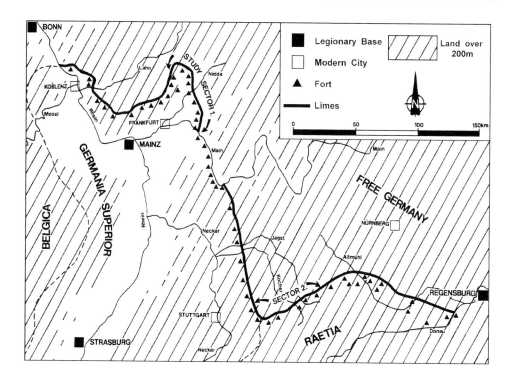

*49 The German* Limes

Burn, and even has its own small exterior bath block. Very little excavation has taken place on these sites using modern methods, and their history remains something of a mystery (but see Seitz 1989). The 'best guess', and it really is little more than a guess, of German archaeologists is that the bulk of the *Kleinkastelle* are Trajanic or Hadrianic (Mackensen 1988 and Czysz 1977), but some may be earlier or later. It is certainly unclear whether the fortlets were built as part of a single scheme, or added piecemeal over time, and the history of the *Limes*' forts is almost equally problematic. Under these circumstances, it is not always possible to say with certainty exactly which installations were occupied at any one time before the *Limes* reached its final form. This means that any attempt to trace the evolution of the signalling system through the various stages of the frontier's own development, along the lines already followed on Hadrian's Wall, would currently require too much speculation to be of value. So, although I shall have more to say about the dating of the forts at the end of this chapter, the present survey will, otherwise, confine itself to a study of the *Limes* as it existed at its zenith in the mid to late second century AD. It is to be hoped that this situation can some day be rectified, but for the moment we must accept the *Limes*' limitations as a study target for want of any other choice.

Like Hadrian's Wall, the German *Limes* was too large to be studied in its entirety with the resources available and so, initially at least, a single sample study sector was chosen. Unlike on Hadrian's Wall, however, this sector was selected on practical as much as archaeological grounds. One of the principal features of the *Limes* today is the dense forest through which much of the line passes and in which the visual study of site intervisibilities becomes impossible. The sector chosen, therefore, was the area between the tower known as Watch Post (WP) 4/47, in the north-western Wetterau (north of Frankfurt), and the fort of Groß Krotzenburg on the north bank of the River Main (**49 & 50**). This is one of the only continuous stretches of the line both long enough to act as a significant sample of the whole and largely free of modern forest. The sector is 63km (43 Roman miles) long (14 per cent of the whole) and runs around the whole of the northern and eastern sides of the Wetterau basin. It includes 96 separate installations, including eight forts (Arnsburg, Inheiden, Echzell, Ober-Florstadt, Altenstadt, Marköbel, Rückingen and Groß Krotzenburg) and 14 *Kleinkastelle* and has the additional advantage of being part of the original, Trajanic (once thought to be Domitianic, but see Körtüm 1998) Rhine-Main system: the only part of the *Limes* in which the entire developmental history of the frontier took place on the same line. It does, however, have a number of shortcomings as a truly representative sample. Firstly, it lies wholly within the province of Germania Superior, and secondly the terrain is here rather more gentle than is common on other parts of the system. As a control, therefore, the entire remainder of the line was either walked or driven and a second sector (**49**) was surveyed in detail. The latter lay further to the south-east at the point where the system crosses the Upper German-Raetian border, an area, also now largely free of forest, but which does show rather more rugged terrain. This second survey will be dealt with separately in chapter 5, however, and the current chapter will now deal exclusively with the Wetterau sector.

At first sight the study sector appears fairly homogenous, both within itself and with the rest of the system. The frontier is arranged in its usual configuration with all of its installations, including the forts, arranged a little behind the line and, so far as is known, there are no outposts of any sort. The line itself initially consisted only of a road, later reinforced with a timber palisade and later still with a ditch and earth rampart, now known as the 'Pfahlgraben' (**51**). The forts stand at reasonably regular intervals of about 6-7km ($4\frac{1}{2}$ Roman miles). But, unlike the turrets of Hadrian's Wall, the watchtowers have no regular spacing system and their intervals vary from less than 500m to more than a kilometer. They are, however (again unlike Hadrian's Wall's turrets), always positioned so as to be intervisible with both of their immediate neighbours and this seems to have been an important enough factor in their siting to cause at least some of the spacing variations. Over much of the area the *Kleinkastelle* give the initial impression of being built almost at random. Their average spacing over the sector is 4.5km (3 Roman miles), but this conceals a situation in which their spacings can vary from 1.2km (0.8 Roman miles), between KK Wingertsberg and KK Massohl, near Inheiden, to 10.5km (7 Roman miles) between KK Buchkopf and KK Langendiebach around the fort of Marköbel.

What does not appear to have been noticed before, however, is that on closer inspection the study sector breaks down quite neatly into two. The break occurs around WP 4/94 and results in northern (Arnsburg-Ober-Florstadt) and southern (Altenstadt-Groß Krotzenburg) zones, of 35 and 28km ($23\frac{1}{2}$ and 19 Roman miles) respectively, each of which contains four of the eight forts, but which otherwise show markedly different characteristics. These are most apparent on the ground, but even on relatively small scale maps (**50, 52 & 59**) three important differences should be visible.

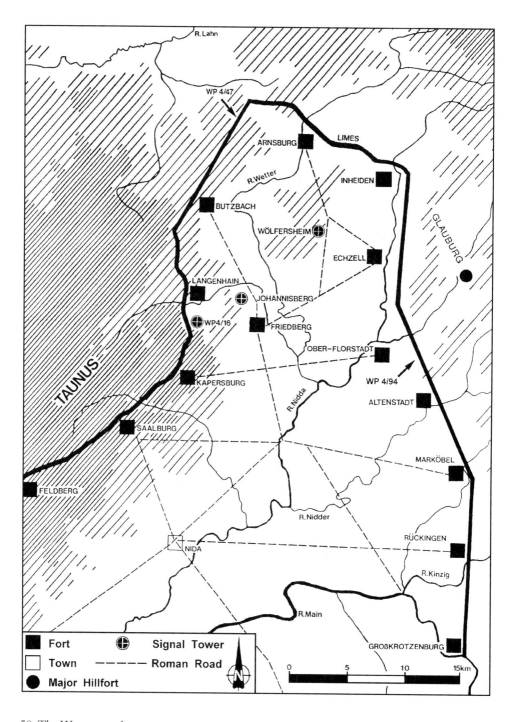

*50 The Wetterau study sector*

*51 The Pfahlgraben, with reconstructed palisade*

1   Whilst the forts lie behind the *Limes*, throughout the study sector, rather than being attached to it, those of the southern zone stand almost immediately behind the line, separated from it by only a matter of metres. In the north, however, the forts can be much further back. Arnsburg and Echzell, for example, are both around 1.5 km (just over a Roman mile) behind the frontier and Ober-Florstadt is more than 2.5 km (1.7 Roman miles) from the *Limes*. Even Inheiden is probably at least 400m from the line, but the exact course of the frontier is somewhat uncertain at this point. Furthermore, whilst the northern forts are often built on high and/or prominent ground, those of the southern zone tend to be low-lying.

2   *Kleinkastelle* are much more common and lie closer together in the north. The southern sector has four of these fortlets in 28km, an average spacing of 7km. But the north has 10 in 35km, an average spacing of only 3.5km, which falls to just 3.2km when we consider that the first installation outside the north-western limit of the study sector (KK Holzheimer Unterwald) is also a *Kleinkastell*.

3   The *Limes* runs much straighter in the south than in the north. The entire 28km run of the southern zone is formed by just two almost perfectly straight sections, which hinge together at the fort of Marköbel. The more northerly of these two straights then carries on for a short distance into the northern zone, as far as KK Lochberg. But thereafter, the *Limes* makes frequent twists and turns right around the northern Wetterau until it reaches WP 4/48a, just before the point where the study sector ends.

It then lines up into another long straight to run on past the fort of Butzbach. Over much of this zone the *Limes* is, of course, turning anyway, to form the northern Wetterau loop, so that some changes of direction are inevitable. But this does not explain the frequency and nature of the turns. The overall 180 degree bend of the Wetterau loop takes place on the grossest scale of frontier layout. It extends over almost 20km and is barely appreciable on the ground. Within this area, however, the *Limes* makes many sharper turns, some of which run against the general trend of the loop.

A fourth difference between the two zones, closely related to number 3 above and only really appreciable on the ground, is their relative tactical positions. In the southern zone, with its long straight runs, the *Limes* appears to take no account whatever of the terrain through which it passes. The rolling countryside offers considerable tactical opportunities which could have been exploited quite easily had small deviations in the overall line been allowed. Yet the *Limes* ploughs on, remorselessly straight. In doing so it puts itself into some absurd tactical positions, often facing steeply rising ground immediately outside the line, so that many of the watchtowers have extremely limited views forward and a few even have poor views along their immediate sector of the frontier line itself. Either the designers of this sector had no interest in tactical considerations or, for some reason, the *Limes* needed to be straight here even more than it needed to be strong.

In the northern sector, on the other hand, although the ground is virtually identical, rolling farmland with frequent broad but low hills, the layout of the frontier is very different. Here the priority seems to have been to exploit the full tactical potential of the terrain, and so the *Limes* runs from high point to high point, changing course frequently in pursuit of this aim. The result is that the frontier here follows a very much stronger line than in the south and, as most of the high points are occupied by watchtowers or *Kleinkastelle*, its installations tend to have much better views out into barbarian territory than their southern counterparts, despite the fact that in both sectors much of the frontier faces more mountainous country at fairly close range.

A number of areas remain puzzling, however, despite (or perhaps because of) the obvious care with which the bulk of the northern sector has been laid out. For amongst all this strength, there are one or two short stretches where the *Limes* follows a weak tactical line, offering poor vantage points, when much stronger ground was available close, sometimes very close, by (for example the area from KK Feldheimer Wald to WP 4/71). Most peculiar of all, however, are the positions of some of the watchtowers. As has already been said, the *Limes* in this area exploits the high points and it is usual for the hilltops to be occupied by towers or *Kleinkastelle*, which thus enjoy the strongest possible positions and the best possible vantage points. Occasionally, however, the towers (and *Limes*) have been built some way below the summit on the inside, or Roman face, of a hill. This means that instead of occupying the commanding position available, often very close by, the installation sits on weak ground and is deprived of any view forward except straight into the hillside. We have already seen that there is no rigid spacing system at work on this frontier and there appear to be no constructional reasons for these oddities, as these gentle hills would have presented no difficulties to Roman military builders. On the face of it, therefore, it is almost as if these installations have been quite deliberately, and seriously, weakened. But these are exactly the sorts of oddities which have provided our insights into the workings of Hadrian's Wall, and the time has come to turn to the intervisibility data.

## The signalling system

Almost all thinking on the signalling system of the German *Limes* has hitherto been dominated by the simple fact of its minor installations (towers and *Kleinkastelle*) being universally intervisible with their immediate neighbours. As a result, the assumption has grown up, even more strongly than had been the case on Hadrian's Wall, that signalling must have been carried out laterally, with messages being relayed tower to tower along the frontier line, although interestingly, there is a reconstruction model in the *Limes* museum at Aalen showing an attack on the *Limes* and a watchtower signalling directly back to a fort. It must be admitted from the outset that although such a system would always have been out of the question on Hadrian's Wall, where the minor installations are not all intervisible with their neighbours, it would have been perfectly possible on the *Limes*. But this does not necessarily mean that this was what was actually done.

Unfortunately, there are no written sources to tell us how the frontier worked and, as signalling procedures leave only the most tenuous of physical traces, there are obvious limitations to a purely archaeological approach. A survey like this can thus only examine the physical remains of frontier installations to determine what was feasible, given their particular layout, and this may result in a range of possible options. The traditionally envisaged lateral approach to signalling is certainly inefficient, and there is a natural tendency to assume that the most efficient system of which a given set of installations were capable was the one actually in use. But this is probably impossible to prove and again we must accept that because the *Limes* is capable of operating a lateral signalling system, it is quite possible that it actually did so, even if more efficient systems also prove to have been practicable. Nevertheless, as has already been stated, lateral signalling is so inefficient that to rely on such a system would constitute poor military practice and, in view of what is to follow, it is worthwhile examining in a little more depth why this is so.

To be effective, any military communications system, of whatever size or historical period, must fulfil certain basic criteria. Firstly, of course, it must work and, secondly, it must be as efficient as possible which, in practical terms, means that it must transmit as much information as possible, as quickly and reliably as possible, whilst using as little manpower (especially skilled manpower), energy and capital equipment as possible. These criteria do, of course, also apply to civilian systems. But a military system must also strive to be as invulnerable as possible to enemy attack. This means that, even more than a civilian system, which merely has to protect itself against human and equipment failure, military signalling must contain fail-safe mechanisms, duplications and parallelisms which will allow the system as a whole to survive the destruction of at least some of its component parts. Naturally, other precautions can also be taken, such as protecting or physically hardening individual signalling sites, or by building them, where possible, in inaccessible places. Nevertheless, other things being equal, the greater the level of redundancy (duplication) a well-designed system contains, the greater the level of punishment the system will be able to withstand before it will fail, and so the more effective and reliable it will be under combat conditions. A classic example here is the Internet, which began life as a military system, which exploits a decentralised architecture and frequent duplication to produce a system that was designed to withstand a nuclear attack by re-routing data around any parts of its own infrastructure that had failed or suffered destruction.

If we now return to the specific case of Roman frontier design, we can apply these criteria to the two basic choices of possible signalling system available: the traditionally envisaged lateral system and the direct system seen on Hadrian's Wall, in which, ideally, every minor installation is linked directly to a fort or other strategic site. Obviously both systems can be made to work, and so both fulfil the first qualification. But the direct system is much more efficient in two distinct ways. Firstly, it operates faster, as most signals do not need relaying before they reach their goal. Secondly, even when transmitting little more than alarm beacons, this type of system also conveys more information, simply because, as the signals are direct, the recipients can see, and thus identify, their source. This means that, whilst the slow, lateral system could only inform a fort that there was trouble, the faster direct system could also tell it where that trouble was. If more complex code carrying systems were also in use on the frontiers, the direct system acquires the further advantage that, as signals pass through fewer hands on the way to their destination, there is far less risk of their being garbled in transmission, reception or relay. But a direct system is also far less vulnerable to enemy action. Because the lateral system needs to pass information via each tower between its source and the nearest fort, an enemy has only to neutralise a single tower for the whole system to fail. On the level of local alarm signals this may not be quite as serious as it sounds because most installations lie somewhere between two forts, and a signal blocked in one direction may still get through in the other. But the frontier installations of such a system would also have to carry the longer-range strategic traffic between the forts themselves and this would be totally disrupted by such an incident. On a direct system, however, the destruction of any one minor installation would make no difference whatsoever to any of the others. Indeed, because the links are direct, each site's communications are totally independent and it would be theoretically possible for a single surviving tower, anywhere within a particular fort's sphere of influence, to retain unimpaired contact with that fort despite the destruction of every other installation on the sector. The weakness in the inter-fort chain continues to exist, of course, simply because this does usually still have to be operated using relays. Nevertheless, the direct system is superior even here, because, as we shall see below, it can only be put out of action by the destruction of certain specific installations, which can be protected and/or duplicated, whilst the lateral system can be disabled by the neutralisation of any installation. It should thus be readily apparent that lateral signalling systems contain dangerous inherent weaknesses and it seems likely that any sensible military organisation would strive to avoid them. Should we find such a system actually installed on a Roman frontier, therefore, it would seem reasonable to conclude that, for some reason, no alternative was possible.

It is worth noting at this point, however, that both these models represent somewhat idealised positions and it is unlikely that either system would ever be found in a completely pure state on a real Roman frontier. Even in a direct system it will often be impossible to give every single minor installation a direct link with a fort and so a few sites may still require relays. Likewise, on a lateral system, we could still probably expect quite a number of installations to be directly intervisible with a fort, especially those in its immediate vicinity. What we are likely to observe in the field, therefore, are hybrid systems which tend towards one extreme or the other whilst containing elements of both. Nevertheless, it should still be readily apparent to which class of system a given example belongs.

## The northern zone

We can now turn to the actual position on the Wetterau *Limes* study sector, and once again the area breaks neatly into the same northern and southern zones we saw earlier, with very different signalling systems possible in each. The system in the northern zone appears to be a direct system (**52**), almost identical to that of the Stanegate phase of Hadrian's Wall (*see* **25**). The configuration of the two frontiers is obviously very similar with the forts set well back from the line itself and so are the results, for almost every minor installation in the zone enjoys direct intervisibility with a fort. There is one obvious difference between the two frontiers, in that the *Limes* lacks the Stanegate/Hadrian's Wall combination's rearward relay towers (Mains Rigg, Barcombe etc.), which could have improved its situation still further. But, even without this provision, only five of the zone's 51 minor installations (KK Grüningen and Langsdorf, and WP 4/63, 4/65 and 4/67/8) require relays to signal to a fort. In every case the relay needed is a simple one-stage affair via just one other site. Furthermore, although for convenience **52** shows these sites being relayed by one specific neighbour, none of the five are actually dependent on just a single relay site. All have a choice of at least two and sometimes more. This is important as a safety feature, because it means that none of these installations can be cut off by the destruction of any one other site. In view of the terrain through which the *Limes* passes, this is a very considerable achievement (especially since it is not absolutely certain that the three watchtowers needing relays actually exist) and it is obvious on the ground that a very great deal of care and skill have gone into the laying out of this area. The constantly undulating country and low gentle hills, whilst presenting no real difficulties to the builders of the system, must have been a nightmare from the signaller's point of view. Yet the frontier has been threaded through it in such a way as to facilitate communications whilst still providing most of the watchtowers with suitable view points and keeping the line as a whole tactically strong.

Some concessions have had to be made to the terrain, however, and the sites not enjoying direct links to a fort seem to have been the victims. For although all five could have been avoided, this could only have been done at the cost of major deviations of the line. For example, four of the five form a tight group around WP 4/64 (**52, 53 & 55**) which serves to link them all to the fort at Arnsburg. Three of these sites (WP 4/65, KK Langsdorf and WP 4/67/8) lie in a broad dip to the east of WP 4/64, between it and KK Feldheimer

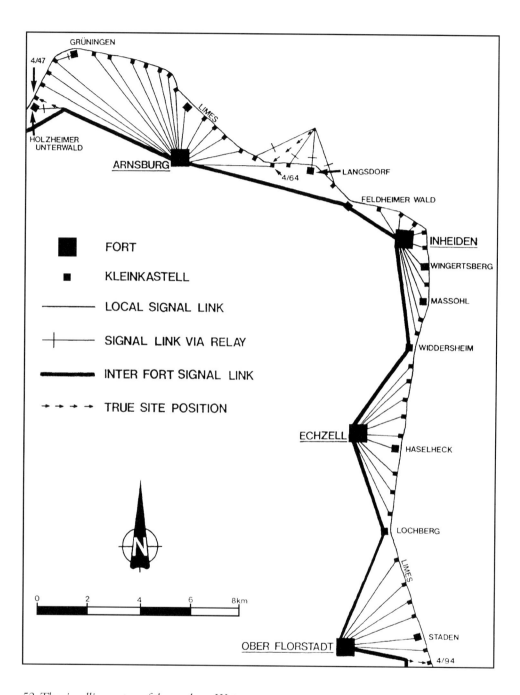

GRÜNINGEN

4/47

HOLZHEIMER
UNTERWALD

LIMES

ARNSBURG

4/64

LANGSDORF

FELDHEIMER WALD

INHEIDEN

WINGERTSBERG

MASSOHL

WIDDERSHEIM

ECHZELL

HASELHECK

LOCHBERG

LIMES

STADEN

OBER FLORSTADT

4/94

■ FORT

■ KLEINKASTELL

—— LOCAL SIGNAL LINK

—+— SIGNAL LINK VIA RELAY

━━ INTER FORT SIGNAL LINK

→ → → → TRUE SITE POSITION

N

0    2    4    6    8km

*52 The signalling system of the northern Wetterau zone*

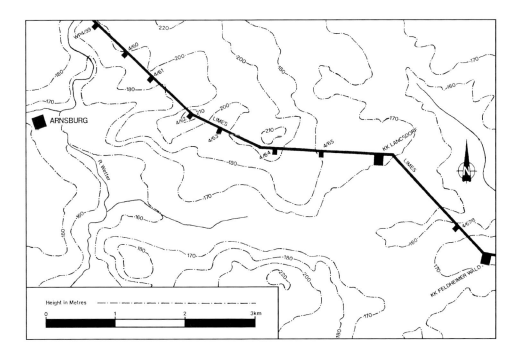

*53 The Arnsburg-Feldheimer Wald sector*

Wald, and are cut off from the fort by the hill on which WP 4/64 itself stands. The remaining tower (WP 4/63) lies in a smaller dip to the west of WP 4/64 and is cut off from Arnsburg by the hill carrying its western neighbour WP 4/62. It would have been perfectly possible to reroute the *Limes* so that more, or even all, of these sites could have seen the fort, but only at the cost of installing two deep and rather wasteful re-entrants at this point. This would have lengthened the line as well as bringing it down onto lower and much weaker ground from which its installations would have had a poor view forward.

Likewise, KK Grüningen (**54 & 56**) stands in a pronounced dip between two areas of stronger ground right at the north-western tip of the Wetterau loop. This small pass provides a natural route into and out of Roman territory and the O.R.L. (Abt A, Band II, 2, Tafel 7.6 and Karte 4 & 7 plus Abt B, Band II, 2, Nr 15) shows suspected Roman roads approaching it from the south and south-east. It certainly still carries a modern road and the need to supervise such a route with an installation of some power might explain the unusually large size of the fortlet (*c*.2900m$^2$). But the site also has higher ground some way to its rear and is thus cut off from Arnsburg. Once more the situation could have been avoided only at the cost of either another deep local re-entrant, or of pulling the entire line in the vicinity back by about 500m, from its present fairly strong position where much of it follows a ridge top, onto lower and much less satisfactory ground.

As well as allowing these purely local links between the individual line installations and their nearest forts, the northern zone is also well designed to facilitate communications between the forts themselves. Indeed, once again, the efficiency of this longer range,

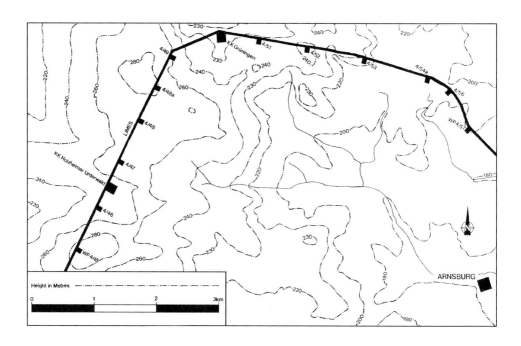

*54  The Arnsburg-Grüningen sector*

*55  The view north-west from KK Feldheimer Wald to WP 4/64 (1) and KK Langsdorf (2) and Arnsburg (3)*

*56 The view north from WP 4/49 to KK Grüningen (1). The* Limes *follows the curving hedgerow towards the wooded hill (2). Arnsburg fort is out of shot to the right*

strategic or inter-fort system compares well with the various phases of the Tyne-Solway frontier in Britain. Unlike both the Stanegate (where Castle Hill can see Old Church Brampton) and the Wall fort phase of Hadrian's Wall (where Housesteads can see Carrawburgh) none of the *Limes* forts are actually intervisible. But, on the other hand, whereas Housesteads and Great Chesters on Hadrian's Wall needed to use a double relay (via T 40b and Barcombe B) in order to signal to each other, all four of the northern zone *Limes* forts can communicate with their neighbours by means of single relay sites. If we take just those inter-fort links which lie wholly within the northern zone, Arnsburg is linked to Inheiden via KK Feldheimer Wald, Inheiden to Echzell via KK Widdersheim, and Echzell can signal to Ober-Florstadt via KK Lochberg (**57**). The links between Arnsburg and the fort of Butzbach, which lies beyond the western limit of the northern zone, and between Ober-Florstadt and Altenstadt, in the southern sector (**50, 52 & 59**), are more complicated, however, and we will return to these in a moment.

Again like Hadrian's Wall, this northern zone also shows very clearly defined spheres of responsibility for each of the forts. In most cases, the site which serves as the relay link between two forts stands on particularly prominent ground which actually blocks any view past it from the sites in either direction. The relay thus becomes the only site common to both forts' fields of view and it is sometimes the case that no other installation in one fort's sector can see any of the sites in those of the neighbouring forts. The northern zone thus comes to resemble a series of linked but otherwise almost independent building blocks or *clausaurae*, each consisting of a fort and a distinct set of frontier installations. These blocks are

*57 The view south from KK Widdersheim to Echzell (1) and KK Lochberg (2)*

tightly integrated internally, but each is connected with its neighbours at only one point. The best example of such a block is the Echzell sector (**52 & 57**). The limits of the fort's sphere of responsibility are defined by the two *Kleinkastelle* at Widdersheim and Lochberg, which serve to link the fort with its two neighbours: Inheiden (**58**) and Ober-Florstadt. Within Echzell's sphere of responsibility all of the minor installations, without exception, can see the fort. But the *Kleinkastelle* themselves stand on such prominent knolls that no other installation within the sector, including the fort, can see past them into either of the blocks beyond. Such a situation obviously has disadvantages in that it increases the system's vulnerability to attack. We have already mentioned the vital role of redundancy in military communications systems. Yet this part of the *Limes'* inter-fort signalling chain contains no redundancy as only the relay *Kleinkastelle* can see into two blocks at once. This means that, unlike the local signalling system, where each of the sites needing relays had a choice of at least two, the two *Kleinkastelle* are the only installations capable of relaying Echzell's signals to its neighbours and the system becomes totally dependent on the survival of these sites. There could, however, have been a slight corresponding advantage because no installation on this block can see anything for which it is not immediately responsible. On such a low technology system, where a signal, once given, would be difficult to countermand, this makes it difficult for any installation to cause confusion by inappropriately initiating signals towards or responding to signals from outside its own sector. There is a close parallel here with the situation of Barcombe B on Hadrian's Wall. For although that tower lies well to the south of the frontier barrier, it serves as the only possible one-stage relay between Housesteads and Vindolanda. It too has been carefully sited so as to be in visual contact with every installation in its own specific sphere of responsibility (T 40b to Housesteads), but nothing whatsoever beyond it.

*58 Inheiden fort (arrowed) from KK Widdersheim*

Finally, there does appear to have been at least some logic behind the *Kleinkastelle* positions in the northern zone. We have already seen that all of the links in the inter-fort signalling chain are provided by *Kleinkastelle* (Lochberg, Widdersheim and Feldheimer Wald), at least where both of the forts so connected lie within the zone. It was obviously sensible to have had such important, yet potentially vulnerable, links protected by these rather stronger installations. There is, therefore, a tendency for the forts to have *Kleinkastelle* as flank markers at the edges of their spheres of responsibility. In addition to this, however, most of the forts have another *Kleinkastell* directly in front of them. For example Ober-Florstadt has KK Staden, Echzell has KK Haselheck, and Arnsburg may have an, as yet unnamed, *Kleinkastell* to its north on the traditional position of WP 4/57 (*see* **52 & 54**), although the evidence is currently still scanty (Kröll & Schönberger 1965). The situation at Inheiden is somewhat less clear, but even this fort has KK Wingertsberg close by to the south-east. It would seem logical that these sites were protecting passages of some sort through the *Limes* which gave the forts' garrisons access to the outside world and they may also have facilitated civilian traffic through the frontier. Unfortunately, however, no definite evidence for such crossing points has yet emerged in the study sector, although KK Degerfeld, the equivalent *Kleinkastell* at the fort of Butzbach (*see* **50**), is known to stand on such a route (Jorns 1967, H.Simon 1968 and Baatz 1971).

The remaining three *Kleinkastelle* on the sector may be a response to specific areas of local weakness, because a number of them stand on weak sections of ground which also lie out of sight of, and so outside the immediate protection of, a fort. We have already seen KK Grüningen guarding a pass to the north-west of Arnsburg, and KK Langsdorf may fulfil a similar role in the blind hollow east of WP 4/64 discussed above (*see* **55**). Another example of this may be KK Holzheimer Unterwald, just outside the north-western end of the study sector, which again stands in a distinct dip and is not in direct contact with a fort (*see* **54**). This installation probably still forms part of Arnsburg's sector of responsibility and its signals can be relayed to the fort via WP 4/47. KK Massohl, to the south-east of Inheiden, is more difficult to explain, however, because although the ground on which it stands is not particularly strong, it is in full view of the fort. Its position is dominated by the neighbouring *Kleinkastelle* of Wingertsberg and Widdersheim, which stand on much stronger ground at close range to either side. One possible answer, in this case, may lie in the fact that Inheiden is only a small Numerus fort, not a full cohort or *ala* base like the other forts in the zone. The concentration of *Kleinkastelle* in its vicinity may, therefore, be nothing more than an attempt to harden up a potential weak spot, although this is little more than a guess.

## The southern zone

The parallels between the northern zone of the Wetterau study sector and the Tyne Solway frontier are clear to see and the case for elements of a universal design, if not exactly proven, becomes considerably more attractive. In the southern zone, however, things are very different and the signalling system veers much more towards a lateral arrangement (**59**). As a proportion of the whole, three times as many installations cannot see a fort as on the northern sector: 10 out of 34 (30 per cent) as opposed to 5 out of 51 (10 per cent), and one installation, WP 5/13, needs a double relay via two other sites before its signals would reach the fort of Groß Krotzenburg. This situation is bad enough, but it would have been far worse if not for a gift of the terrain. The *Limes* in this sector crosses a series of four river valleys, roughly at right angles (**60**), and all four forts stand on low ground close to the rivers, so that Groß Krotzenburg stands besides the Main, Rückingen beside the Kinzig, Marköbel the Krebs Bach, and Altenstadt not far from the Nidder. As a result of this, many of the minor installations stand on higher ground on the valley sides and can see down to the forts. Nevertheless, the situation could have been made very much better, with comparatively little effort, if not for the line's rigid straightness which, as we have seen, also weakened it tactically in this zone. For had the *Limes* been allowed to follow a stronger, more twisting course, to exploit the terrain as it does further north, more sites could have been brought into positions intervisible with a fort. The situation is further weakened by the fact that all of the forts in the zone are built so close to the frontier line.

On both the northern zone of the present study sector and the Stanegate phase of Hadrian's Wall, the fact that the forts are set well back from the line, usually on high, or at least highly visible, ground is of considerable help in ensuring that the maximum number of frontier installations could see them. We have already seen that when the Wall forts were built on the line of Hadrian's Wall a large number of sites lost their direct view to a fort and the configuration and problems of the southern Wetterau zone are exactly the same. A good example can be seen at Marköbel, where the fort lies in a loop of the river Krebs Bach, close behind the *Limes*, at an altitude of just under 130m (**59-61**).

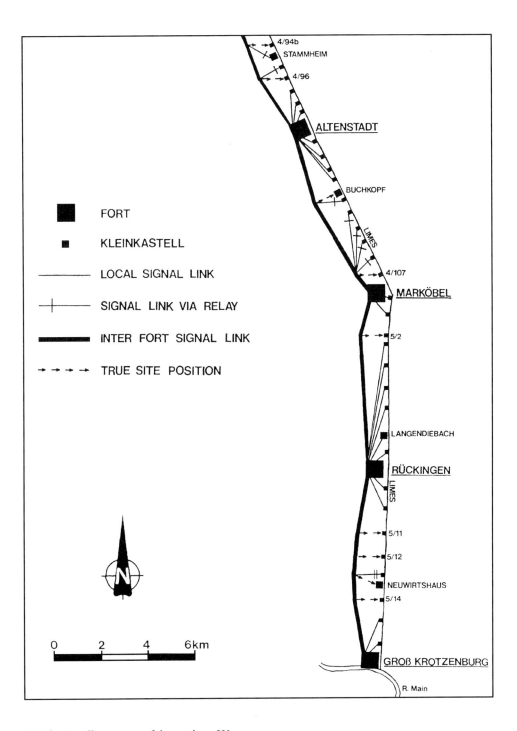

*59 The signalling system of the southern Wetterau zone*

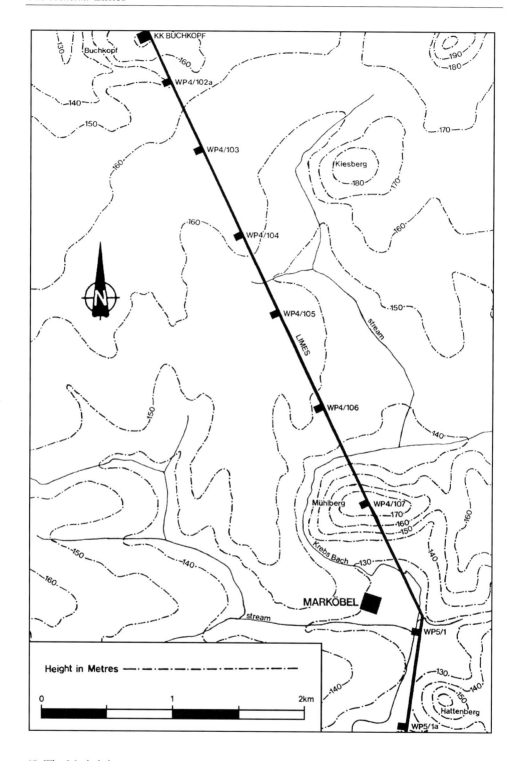

*60 The Marköbel area*

*61 Mühlberg (1) and Marköbel (2) from WP 5/2*

Immediately to the north, on the opposite bank of the river, the ground rises abruptly to just under 180m to form the steep but compact hill known as the Mühlberg (**61 & 62**), on the summit of which stands WP 4/107. This hill totally blocks the fort's view to the north, which means that it can only signal north via WP 4/107. Yet, had Marköbel been built just a few hundred metres further back, on the slightly higher ground to its west, it would have been able to see behind the Mühlberg (**62**). This would have given the fort a greatly enhanced view to the north (**63**), stretching some 5km to the summit of the next major hill, the Buchkopf (height 170m), and would have made it intervisible with all of the block of five, currently blind, sites between KK Buchkopf and WP 4/107. This one simple layout change could have halved the number of installations requiring relays in the southern zone to a proportion little worse than that in the north; yet for some reason the opportunity was ignored.

The design of the southern zone, as it affects the local tower-fort signalling system, is thus certainly curious. It could so easily have been made better and, in less forgiving country, it might have been very much worse. But it is with the longer range, inter-fort system that the area's weaknesses really begin to show. Again none of the forts are intervisible. But, unlike the northern zone, only one of the inter-fort links is accomplished by means of a single relay, this being the link between Marköbel and Rückingen, which runs via WP 5/2 (**59 & 64**). Of the remaining inter-fort connections within the zone, the link between Altenstadt and Marköbel needs a double relay, via KK Buchkopf and WP 4/107 (although it could have been accomplished by the *Kleinkastell* alone had Marköbel been in the rearward position discussed above), whilst any signals between Rückingen and Groß Krotzenburg would have needed to pass through no less than four relay sites. Furthermore, the link between Altenstadt and the fort of Ober-Florstadt in the northern

62  *The Mühlberg (1) and the southern part of Marköbel village (2) from the* Limes *line to its north*

63  *The view north from WP 4/107 to KK Buchkopf (arrowed)*

*64 Telephoto view south from WP 5/2 to Rückingen (arrowed)*

zone also requires a double relay via WP 4/94b and 4/96. It is true that some degree of thought seems to have gone into these links. For example, WP 5/2 has been sited on high ground only about one third of the average tower interval from WP 5/3, presumably to facilitate the connection between Marköbel and Rückingen, but the system is still very inefficient. Moreover, as the neutralisation of any of these relay sites would have cut the inter-fort chain, it is also vulnerable to disruption by enemy action. Yet although we have seen the, anyway lesser, vulnerability of the simpler northern inter-fort system countered by the use of *Kleinkastelle* for the relay stations, the southern relays are mostly ordinary watchtowers. Indeed, there seems to be no logic at all behind the siting of the few *Kleinkastelle* to be found in the south as they do not appear able to fulfil any of the roles marked out for them further north. It is also much more difficult to discern clear borders between the spheres of responsibility of the forts in the southern zone, especially in the sector between Rückingen and Groß Krotzenburg.

We are obviously confronted with a problem here. We have taken a reasonably representative sample of an apparently homogeneous Roman frontier system. We have seen that throughout its 63km length this sample is made up of the same basic building blocks, runs through similar terrain, faces much the same hill country outside the line, and is uniformly backed by the same rolling Wetterau farmland. Yet, on closer inspection, our study sector breaks down into two distinct zones which, despite belonging to the same building period, appear to have very different layouts and operating systems. Furthermore, whilst one of these systems is secure, logical and efficient, the other appears to be clumsy and potentially vulnerable. Such a situation cannot be accidental and it thus requires explanation. For example, if the southern system had operated throughout the whole of the study sector, we could simply have argued that, as this is a very early system, Roman frontier design was still in an unsophisticated state and that by the time of the slightly later Hadrian's Wall/Stanegate combination ideas had advanced sufficiently for a more efficient system to be produced. But the two *Limes* zones exist side by side, and are contemporary. Nor can we argue that what we are seeing in the Wetterau is a process of learning, with the *Limes* builders starting out from Groß Krotzenburg using one design, then realising, by the time they reached WP 4/94, that what they were building was flawed and improving that design. For, in the north-western limits of the present study sector, south of WP 4/49, the *Limes* returns to an identical configuration to that of the southern zone and once again begins to run on a perfectly straight course, which it holds for almost 11km until it reaches WP 4/33, about 1.5km to the south of Butzbach fort. Once this straight sector passes out of sight of Arnsburg, at WP 4/47, it again appears to have adopted a semi-lateral signalling system. All of the line installations between WP 4/38 and 4/45 would have needed their signals relaying to Butzbach via WP 4/37 and the inter-fort link between Arnsburg and Butzbach requires a triple relay via WP 4/47, 4/45 and 4/37. Furthermore, if we look elsewhere on the German frontier, we can find the same two patterns repeated in other sectors, not just on the Trajanic Rhine-Main and Odenwald lines and not just in Germania Superior but even on the later, Antonine, Outer and Raetian limites.

Another approach might be to suggest that the two study sector zones reflect the different ideas and techniques of two different designers or military units working within a fairly loose overall plan. We might perhaps suggest that the zones were built by two different legions, one of which had rather more initiative than the other, and the possibility of alternating legionary building stretches might also explain the recurrence of a lateral arrangement in the contemporary Butzbach sector. Unfortunately, although there are large numbers of building inscriptions and unit brick stamps to commemorate later construction on the frontier, no record survives of the original builders. But, again, the two patterns survive on the Antonine parts of the line. Although it is true that when these were built there were still legions in the area that had been there in Trajanic times, it seems most unlikely that any unit would have been allowed to perpetuate obviously inefficient methods for so long. If one legion's ideas proved markedly inferior to another's, one would expect it to have been disabused of those ideas very quickly. One would also have expected the *Limes* to have been designed as a single whole, even if individual sections were built by different units. This certainly seems to have been the case on Hadrian's Wall, where the system operates in the same way regardless of which unit built a particular sector. In any case, the *Limes* has not yet been shown to exhibit any of the diagnostic differences in installation design that mark the legionary building stretches on the British frontiers. It would seem obvious, therefore, that whatever the forces were that caused the emergence and concurrent operation of two different frontier designs on the Trajanic, Wetterau *Limes*, they were still operating a generation later in the Antonine period.

One example of such a constant might be the strategic position of the area, and it is certainly true (as can be seen from any map of the modern rail and autobahn systems) that it has always been easier to enter (or leave) the Wetterau from the north than from the east.

This is largely due to the presence of the Fulda Gap, a pass through the hill and mountain country which surrounds the Wetterau on its north, east and west sides. This major route way leads from Giessen, just to the north of the Wetterau loop, deep into northern Germany and, as it was also the principle route from the Rhineland into the territory of the former DDR, it still had strategic importance in modern times. We might, therefore, suggest that the northern zone of the study sector was designed to be more efficient, simply because it straddled the most likely invasion route into the area and that the design of the southern zone could be relatively neglected because it did not. This strategic picture is undoubtedly valid and its effects could be seen until recently in the huge concentration of NATO forces that were stationed in the area to block any Soviet invasion of Western Europe through the DDR. It is also true that the Roman army was quite well aware of the Wetterau's potential as a trouble spot and that this had an influence over their military dispositions and strategic planning for the area. An invasion route is a two-way passage and the Romans had already used this route themselves, in their invasions of free Germany in the Augustan and early Tiberian periods. Likewise, the concentration of Augustan and Tiberian military installations in the Wetterau show their continued concern with the region, as did the presence of a double legionary fortress at Mainz throughout the rest of the Julio/Claudian period. The Flavian period also saw a military build-up in the area, as part of wider operations east of the Rhine, so that by the time that the *Limes* was built, there were already forts in its immediate hinterland (Baatz & Herrmann 1989, 69ff). When, in time, these were largely replaced by a new series of forts on the frontier itself, the resulting troop concentration was unparalleled anywhere else on the *Limes* and remained so throughout the frontier's existence. Indeed, it is probably true to say that there were at least as many Roman soldiers per square kilometre in the second-century Wetterau as anywhere else in the Empire, including Hadrian's Wall.

The Wetterau loop, as a whole, is something of a design oddity. It is usually assumed that the Flavian, and later Antonine, advances in Germany stemmed, at least in part, from a desire to shorten the Empire's long northern frontier by cutting off the deep re-entrant formed by the head waters of the Rhine and Danube. The loop could, therefore, be seen as defeating the *Limes*' principal objective, for it lengthens the frontier considerably. A more logical approach would have been to follow the River Main from Mainz to Groß Krotzenburg, thus cutting about 70km off the length of the line. The explanation often given is that the Wetterau is such fertile territory that the Romans would not have been able to resist annexing it. Such considerations may well have been important, but it is debatable whether a desire for land is enough to explain the very northernmost part of the loop. For, had the frontier cut across the Wetterau further south, on a line from Kapersburg through Friedberg to Ober-Florstadt (*see* **50**), it would still have been shorter by about 34km. Yet this would have cost only a relatively small amount of land, much of which is, anyway, somewhat hillier, and so less valuable, than that of the southern Wetterau, and always remained far less densely settled (Baatz & Herrmann, 1982, 85). The loop does, however, have a number of military effects, which might have played some part in the thinking behind its design. Firstly, it brings permanent Roman military bases right up to the mouth of the Fulda gap, whereas the Main lies some 50km to the south. Secondly, it automatically brings a higher troop concentration into the area, simply because given a certain number of forts, and thus men, per unit of frontier length, the greater the length of line laid down in a certain area, the greater will be the number of men who will be stationed there. In other words, simply because the *Limes* loops around the Wetterau rather than running straight across it, it is roughly twice as long as it need have been and so we might expect there to be twice as many forts, and so twice as many men in the area as would have been the case without the loop. In fact, however, there are even more. For the intervals between forts are shorter in the Wetterau than almost anywhere else on the line, and a rather greater proportion than average are full cohort or *ala* bases rather than the *Numeruskastelle* which abound elsewhere. Even this is not the end of the story, however, for behind this densely held line lay still more manpower, in the form of the legionary fortress at Mainz (albeit now reduced to a single legion), and the pre-*Limes* fort of Friedberg, both of which remained in use throughout the *Limes* period. Such a concentration of force, backed by the close proximity of a legion, is exactly the sort of response we might expect to an obvious point of strategic weakness. The shape of the loop means that any raiding party that penetrated the *Limes* from the north would still have had to run a prolonged gauntlet between the Wetterau forts once inside. But to cite such considerations as an explanation for the differences between the signalling systems of the two study sector zones would still be to fundamentally misunderstand the role of *Limes* systems.

It is now generally accepted that Roman linear frontiers were bureaucratic, rather than exclusively military structures, and that they were designed to monitor, tax and control movement across the frontier, not defend their sectors against major attacks. They were built and manned by the army simply because the army constituted a readily available, and otherwise largely idle, pool of state-employed manpower. But although they contained forts, and were ultimately dependent on the backing in force provided by those forts, they are best seen in isolation from them. Whilst it is true that the invasion defence of any Roman province rested upon the units contained in its forts and fortresses, it was largely a matter of convenience that so many of these were situated on the frontiers where their men would also be available for more mundane border duties. In short, Roman frontier lines are militarily indefensible and had little or no strategic role to play. Indeed, it is arguable whether they even had much of a tactical role (perhaps as an early warning system for major incursions). As we saw in chapter 3, any attack in force should have been detected by patrolling and intelligence work long before it came within sight of a frontier watchtower. Furthermore, there is very little evidence that other Roman frontiers either enhanced the quality of their signalling systems around danger spots, or that they in any way relaxed them in strategically less sensitive areas. On Hadrian's Wall, for example, there are great strategic differences between the Irthing Gap and the crags which run for many miles to its east. Yet their signalling systems are identical (chapter 2) and it is also worth noting that of the two most northerly forts in the Wetterau loop one, Inheiden, is only a *Numeruskastell*. In any case, the particular strategic weakness of the northern Wetterau is only relative. For there are also a number of significant routes into the eastern side of the region, most notably the Main Valley itself and the smaller Kinzig Valley, both of which are in the southern zone. The Main has always been a major route way and remains so today, whilst the Kinzig Valley now carries Autobahn 66 and the modern railway from Hanau to Fulda, both of which pass through the *Limes* close to the fort at

Rückingen. From a strategic point of view, both these routes were obviously taken seriously by the Romans. Even in the Flavian period the bulk of the Wetterau forts were grouped around the Main and Nidda (Baatz & Herrmann 1989, 78) whilst, in the *Limes* period, the frontier continued south-east of Groß Krotzenburg along the west bank of the Main itself. These so-called 'Wet Sector' forts may thus have served as a form of defence in depth protecting the Wetterau from attacks along the Main Valley as well as simply monitoring traffic actually crossing the river. It is also worth noting that, throughout the *Limes* period, the legion responsible for this area continued to be based opposite the Main mouth at Mainz, rather than moving north to be closer to the Fulda Gap. Again, however, these strategic considerations appear to have had little effect on the design of the *Limes*' signalling system. Both the Main and Kinzig route ways pass through the *Limes* in the southern zone of the study sector, yet neither produced even a local strengthening of the signalling system where it crosses the line. Indeed, quite the reverse, for the stretch of frontier between Rückingen and Groß Krotzenburg is noticeably the least efficient in the entire southern zone (*see* **59**).

It also seems unlikely that more local threats could have had much influence over the study sector's design, for the only obvious sources of potential danger, in the vicinity, were the two major hillforts of Glauberg (*see* **50**) and Dünsberg (*c.*20km to the north-west of the Wetterau loop). These are now known to have been abandoned throughout the *Limes* period (Mildenberger 1978 157ff, Herrmann 1985 & 1986), however, and this may well have been under Roman compulsion, as it seems inconceivable that such powerful centres could have been tolerated so close to the frontier line. Both sites were quickly reoccupied after the *Limes* fell. But, although it is possible that, during their occupation, the Romans would still have felt the need to keep an eye on the abandoned sites, to prevent their misuse, there is little evidence that such concerns affected the structure of the *Limes* itself. For example, because of the proximity of the two sites, it has been argued (Schönberger 1957, Schönberger & Simon 1983 and Baatz & Herrmann 1989, 227f) that the fort of Altenstadt was built specifically to keep watch on Glauberg. But if this is the case it seems odd that there is no corresponding fort aimed at the larger hillfort of Dünsberg. In fact, no special precautions seem to have been taken, for Altenstadt, which is anyway only a *Numeruskastell*, has simply been built at the normal fort spacing interval for the area. The fort stands in a perfectly logical position, guarding the point at which the valley of the River Nidder crosses the frontier, and one would have expected to find it in exactly this position, even if Glauberg did not exist. There also appears to be no link between the hillforts and the differences between the two zones of the study sector's signalling system, for Glauberg lies *c.*6km due west of WP 4/95a in the southern sector, whilst Dünsberg lies facing the northern zone.

There is, however, another possibility. So far we have tended to dismiss the southern zone's layout and signalling system as wholly inferior to that found further north, and certainly by the criteria by which we have been judging, it was. Yet the Romans built it, and continued to build sectors like it throughout the developmental history of the frontier. On the face of it this seems senseless but once again, we must have faith in the judgement of the Roman army. As on Hadrian's Wall, the fact that parts of their military planning strike us as irrational usually means that we have simply not grasped the logic behind them. If we assume, therefore, that the Romans would not deliberately build an inferior system, let alone perpetuate it when a better one was available at no great extra effort, we must conclude that we have misjudged the position. By whatever criteria the Romans were employing, the system was not inferior, or at least, since both systems continued to be used side by side, under certain circumstances it was not inferior. In other words, however paradoxical it may at first appear, there must have been circumstances where the apparently weak southern system could outperform the supposedly much stronger northern system.

Theoretically, the northern zone's direct signalling system is so superior that it is hard to think of any circumstances in which a lateral system would be built in preference to it. But, need the fact that something was built necessarily imply that it was actually preferred? A more likely scenario is that under certain conditions, however much the direct system might be preferable, the lateral system was all that was possible, and once this point is reached an explanation suggests itself immediately, especially in a German context. Naturally, the author cannot claim that it is necessarily correct, but it does, at least, have the virtue of explaining all of the evidence. A direct signalling system does have one potential weakness, in that its successful operation requires a condition which a lateral system does not. Because its signals are passed back from, as well as along, the frontier, a direct system operates in two dimensions and, as Roman signalling depended on clear lines of sight, this means that the system could only function in open country. Yet southern Germany is, and always has been, a land of forests. We have the word of a number of ancient writers for the presence of heavy tree cover here in the Roman period. Just as the author was unable to use visual surveying methods in modern woodland, so a direct signalling system could not have operated in such conditions in ancient times. The Romans were, therefore, faced with a choice between clearing the trees, a massive undertaking, and modifying the system. They may well have opted for the latter, because the great advantage of a lateral system is that, given one proviso, it can operate in forest.

Unlike the direct system, a lateral system operates in one dimension only, because all signalling takes place along the line of the frontier. It has always been assumed that a corridor around the *Limes* would have been kept clear of trees, so as to remove cover and enhance the view of the watchtowers. This means that, so long as the frontier and its installations were confined to a narrow and absolutely straight line, the presence of forest was irrelevant, for the installations could still see down this linear clearing and thus pass their signals freely along it. We would, therefore, expect a frontier system adapted to operate in forest conditions to exhibit a number of characteristic features. Two are essential, and these we have already seen, namely the straight-line path of the frontier and the close proximity of all installations, including the forts, to the line itself. But we might further expect two more. Firstly, where the *Limes* does have to bend it will do so at a fort, so that the fort has the best possible view along both legs of the line; secondly, to allow the relaying of signals, all installations will be intervisible with their immediate neighbours, whatever the effect on spacing (the latter also allows sites to be mutually reinforcing). This is exactly the configuration of the southern zone of the Wetterau study sector and it is particularly noteworthy that the one real bend in this part of the frontier hinges on the fort of Marköbel. The presence of forest would thus explain why the fort was built so close to the *Limes* and not in the position further back from where, as we have seen, it could, in open country, have kept in touch with a much longer section of the line. The obvious conclusion, therefore, is that the southern part of the study sector was forested in Roman times whilst the northern part was not and, interestingly, a broadly similar distribution of woodland can still be seen in the area today.

One further possibility will be dealt with in chapter 5, but the layout of a number of other parts of the line may represent an attempt to cope with forest, whilst still retaining a more direct type of system. For example, at Schwäbisch Gmünd in Raetia, the *Limes* runs along the top of the northern side of a river valley backed by the fort of Schirenhof, which stands high up on the southern slopes, rather than in the valley bottom, as is more normal. Such an arrangement would have allowed the *Limes* to signal over the top of a forested valley and the presence of a group of *Kleinkastelle* in the area, which are intervisible with the fort and can link it with a number of small and otherwise blind lengths of the frontier, may suggest that this was done. Likewise, at the extreme western end of the line, there is a long stretch in which the *Limes* runs along a series of hilltops, whilst the forts lie at quite some distance to the rear, close to the Rhine. For the most part, the two would be intervisible in open country, although modern forestry in the hills means that, in practice, today, they are not. Nevertheless, if we assume that the immediate vicinity of the frontier would have been kept open in Roman times, the forts and frontier installations would again have been able to see and thus exchange signals with each other over the top of any intervening woodland.

This obviously has potential ramifications well beyond the remit of the present study. If we were to succeed in using signalling to set the *Limes* into its environmental context in this area, we could probably do the same for any part of the line. To date, however, such potential must be approached with caution, because insufficient detailed environmental archaeology has been done on the sector to confirm the exact relationship between the frontier and forest at any one point. But we have already seen that the two basic layout types discussed recur at all points and in all periods of the system, and there is a certain amount of environmental data from other sectors which can be tied sufficiently closely to the immediate environs of the frontier line to be of use. This relates to the *Limes* forts of Butzbach, just outside the study sector, and Murrhardt, on the Antonine Outer *Limes* (Streckhan 1958, Knörzer 1973, Knapp 1973 and Rösch 1988), both of which lie on long straight sectors which appear to employ more linear signalling systems. It is encouraging to note, therefore, that in line with our predictions, both these sites were heavily forested in the *Limes* period, as was the fort of Zugmantel in the Taunus mountains, where the frontier might also be expected to use a linear system to cope with the mountainous terrain (Firbas 1930). What is so far lacking, however, is archaeobotanical confirmation of whether any part of the line which appears to be using a direct signalling system lay in open country in Roman times, and until such evidence is forthcoming the relationship between forestry and Roman signalling must remain hypothetical.

The distribution of Romanised agricultural settlement, which could presumably be used as a rough indicator of the contemporary distribution of open farmland, is also of little help in the immediate environs of the frontier itself. For, although the Wetterau can boast an impressive array of Roman villas, especially in the south, there is almost no settlement within the first few kilometres of the *Limes*' hinterland, except for the *vici* around the forts. We are, therefore, left in almost total ignorance about the environment of the immediate frontier area in Roman times. Fortunately, however, this situation may be about to change, thanks to a major study of the ancient environment of the Wetterau which has been established by Dr A. Kreuz of the *Institut für Archäologische Landesforschung* in Hessen. It is to be hoped that her work will soon be able to shed more light on the forest cover of the study sector in Roman times, and the possible use of signalling studies as a tool for environmental archaeology on the frontier should thus be borne in mind.

## Trans-Wetterau signalling

As we have already seen, the Wetterau loop is something of a design anomaly which considerably lengthens the frontier line. It thus seems likely that the Romans would have wanted to shorten the effective length of the frontier for signal communications in just the same way that travelling distances were shortened by driving roads across the base of the loop (*see* **50**). The Wetterau forms a basin which, except for a small area of high ground near Münzenberg, is entirely dominated by the hillier country around its fringes, through which the *Limes* itself runs. This means that many of the frontier installations command superb views over their hinterland, which are often far superior to their views forward or along the line. It is not uncommon for such installations to be able to see right across the Wetterau to the frontier on the opposite side. It is possible, therefore, that the Romans may have attempted to 'short-circuit' the area by transmitting signals from one side of the loop to the other, as well as merely along the line.

The advantages of trans-Wetterau signalling are, perhaps, not as great as might at first sight seem apparent, because the bulk of the signals traffic on a Roman frontier would probably have been between the individual line installations and their nearest fort. Communications of this type were inherently local in nature and thus little affected by larger scale considerations. Nevertheless, the ability to broadcast across the Wetterau loop would have conferred a number of advantages on the frontier's longer range, inter-fort, signalling system. Signalling between forts would probably have served a rather different purpose from the local alert warnings provided by the line installations' signals. For, whilst the latter involved the forts in their day-to-day performance as frontier policing and staffing depots, inter-fort signalling would have enabled large areas of the frontier to be brought rapidly onto a state of alert in times of more general crisis. The inter-fort chain was thus more closely related to the forts' strategic role in the Empire's invasion defences and so, itself, rather more strategic in nature. When seen in this context, trans-Wetterau communications would have given the frontier a threefold advantage. Firstly, by shortening the effective length of the line it would allow still more rapid dissemination of information. Secondly, it would allow the two sides of the Wetterau loop to become mutually reinforcing by enabling each to become a reserve line for the other and, finally, on a more local scale, it would add another element of redundancy into the signalling system. All this, in turn, might go some way towards countering one of the principal inherent dangers of Rome's shallowly held linear frontiers, by allowing the loop to behave, to a certain extent, as a defence in depth.

We have already seen that the defences of the Wetterau area are something of a compromise. The main threat to the region was probably from the north through the Fulda Gap. But, as a number of secondary invasion routes also had to be catered for, the sector's legion was left well to the rear at Mainz, from where it was up to two days' march from the north of the loop. The decision to retain this base was, no doubt, helped by supply considerations and simple inertia. But it also had more positive advantages. For it would have allowed the legion to cover all of the likely invasion routes from a sufficient distance to ensure its freedom of manoeuvre in a crisis, and even to enable it to remain disengaged for long enough to summon further reinforcements should that be necessary. Nevertheless, such a compromise involved dangers because it built a major delay into the effective use of the most important military unit in the area. It would thus have lowered the response time of the system as a whole, especially in a situation that was grave enough to require the defences at maximum strength. The *Limes* itself was manned by a substantial army of auxiliary troops. But, with the sole exception of the unit garrisoning the fort at Friedberg, these were wholly deployed on the actual frontier line and, as we saw in chapter 3, a shallow linear deployment is inherently and seriously vulnerable to a major surprise attack. Roman frontiers were simply not designed to be defended, and although they may look powerful on the ground, if caught by surprise they would have been frighteningly easy to penetrate. As before, one would normally have expected such a system to be well enough screened by intelligence operations for the situation never to arise. For, once warned of a likely attack, the scattered units of a frontier's garrison could regroup to form a powerful field army and thus provide a concentrated and more mobile defence. Even the most ingenious of defences must allow for the human factor, however, for human beings are both resourceful and fallible, and rarely more so than in war. This means that even the most efficient of intelligence systems can fail or be outwitted, and it must be remembered that there appears to have been no outpost system to screen the German *Limes*, as there was on both of the two British Walls. However unlikely such an intelligence failure may have been on the *Limes*, the potential consequences of an unexpected attack in force would have been catastrophic enough to warrant contingency planning and the taking of any available countermeasures. For as we have seen, a linear frontier, once penetrated, is left with its communications disrupted, making further concerted action by the defending forces more difficult.

The very shape of the Wetterau loop would have mitigated these dangers, to a certain extent, by ensuring that any invasion force which penetrated the system down the Fulda Gap from the north would have continued to have forts on its flanks until it was far inside the line, or by forcing the invasion army to divide its forces in order to roll up the defences on either side. Furthermore, the area's configuration makes it likely that the defending units would, for a time, have retained the ability to move parallel with this invasion force, using the frontier's own lateral road. Under these circumstances, trans-Wetterau signal links could have helped to preserve the coherence of the defences, by providing the frontier with a second line of communication, or even by allowing it to signal over the top of the invading forces. The bulk of the system would thus remain fully operational until the invaders had penetrated much further to the south and, as the southern Wetterau was also provided with a good transverse road network (*see* **50**), its defenders would retain the ability to develop properly co-ordinated counterattacks. In effect, therefore, the northern Wetterau could have acted as its own system of outpost forts.

We have already mentioned the fact that a number of ordinary line installations in the northern Wetterau can see right across the loop and are, therefore, theoretically capable of trans-Wetterau signalling. Unfortunately, this brings us into the field of signal protocols which leave no physical trace and with which archaeology is, therefore, ill equipped to deal. But, although such signals cannot be ruled out, they would have been potentially confusing and so, to lessen the risk of small local disturbances triggering a general alert, it seems likely that deliberate transmissions across the loop would have been carried by a special channel using its own dedicated installations. Further south, the distances are anyway greater and relay installations would become essential, simply in order to transmit such signals at all. It is, therefore, these specialist installations for which we should search, for a greater understanding of this subject.

There is currently no evidence for cross-loop signalling in the far south of the Wetterau, for example between the forts of Saalburg and Marköbel or Rückingen. But, as Saalburg has an excellent field of view over its hinterland (stretching right into the heart of modern Frankfurt) and good road links with most of the south-western forts (*see* **50**), the discovery of the relevant relay installations would occasion little surprise. There is, however, a well-established link further north which has the additional merit of integrating the fort of Friedberg (which is not visible from the *Limes*) into the inter-fort signal chain and thus of allowing it to act as a more effective reserve. The evidence for this link takes the form of two abnormally constructed stone towers. Firstly, WP 4/16 (or Gaulskopf) on the *Limes* line at the western side of the loop (**50 & 65**) between the forts of Kapersburg and Langenhain (O.R.L., Abt A, Band II,1, Strecke 4 & 5, 67ff and Abt A, Band II, 2, Strecke 4, Tafel 4, 3), and, secondly, Johannisberg, Bad Nauheim (Helmke 1910), which stands 6.5km inside the line on high ground, to the north of Friedberg (**66**). These towers, whilst not completely identical, form a distinct and contemporary pair which are easily distinguishable from the standard *Limes* towers. They are slightly larger in ground plan and, unlike the usual towers, they seem to have had tiled roofs. But their main distinguishing feature is their massive and heavily buttressed foundations, which suggest that they were significantly taller than normal. Both towers enjoy remarkable fields of view and can, between them, see all of the northern Wetterau forts except Inheiden, as well as being intervisible themselves. WP 4/16 can see Kapersburg, Langenhain, Butzbach, Arnsburg and possibly Saalburg, whilst Johannisberg can signal to Friedberg, Echzell and Ober-Florstadt. This means that almost the whole of the northern Wetterau could be alerted by just these two installations and that cross loop signals could be initiated by all but one of the forts in the area, including Friedberg, which would otherwise have been entirely cut off from the system.

This much is well known, but there is, in fact, a third abnormal tower, *c.*10km to the north-west of Johannisberg at Wölfersheim-Wohnbach (**50 & 67**), whose field of view would appear to have attracted rather less attention. The tower was excavated in 1897 (Kofler 1898) and again found to have been of massive construction and to have had a tiled roof. Unfortunately, the published report contains neither a ground plan nor a proper description of the foundations (which have since been destroyed), but its

*65  A modern reconstruction on the site of WP 4/16, Gaulskopf*

*66 The remains of the Johannisberg tower*

*67 The view north from Johannisberg to Wölfersheim (arrowed)*

identification as a member of the same class of tower seems assured. Wölfersheim stands on one of the tallest hills in the northern Wetterau. But, as it is now surrounded by dense forest, it has proved impossible to make a visual study of its field of view. There is, however, a certain amount of evidence that the area was open country in Roman times, for the site lies amid a small concentration of villas, one of which (Wohnbacher Hinterwald) is less than 800m away. If this was the case, then the site's position was truly magnificent. For, to judge from contour maps and back sighting from the *Limes*, it is potentially intervisible with all four of the northernmost forts of the Wetterau (Butzbach to Echzell), including Inheiden, as well as almost all of this sector of the frontier line itself. It would also have been in contact with Johannisberg and, probably, WP 4/16, so that as well as bringing Inheiden into the system it could have served as a relay point on these towers' (perhaps excessively) long-range links with Arnsburg and Echzell. Taken in concert, therefore, these three abnormal towers would have greatly enhanced the communications of a potentially vulnerable sector, and it is, perhaps, worth considering whether they may also have been instrumental in allowing the whole of the northern Wetterau to be co-ordinated from a single point. Certainly, the advantages of some form of overall command headquarters are not hard to see in such a situation. With its central position at the hub of both the area's road network and of this cross-Wetterau signal system, the *cohors milliaria equitata* base at Friedberg would be an obvious candidate. It should be noted, however, that the three towers of Johannisberg, Wölfersheim and WP 4/16 are not primary. They came relatively late in the frontier's developmental sequence and appear to have been abandoned early. Their earliest pottery dates from the mid-second century AD and Johannisberg contains reused Hadrianic structural material. None of the sites has so far produced either a stone or timber predecessor and, as they seem to have been abandoned around AD 190, their occupation was relatively brief. It is therefore possible that, whatever its theoretical advantages, trans-Wetterau signalling proved, in practice, to be either unsuccessful or unnecessary.

## The fort system

There now remains one more problem to which the study of signalling may be able to make some small contribution, and that is the debated histories of the frontier's forts (Schönberger 1969 & 1985). These are still controversial, but it does, at least, now seem certain that the full unit auxiliary forts and *Numeruskastelle* were later additions to the original plan, some of them considerably later, for Saalburg (O.R.L., Abt. B, Band II, 1, Nr 11 and Abt. A, Band II, 1, Strecke 3, 126ff. Schönberger 1970 and Baatz 1981) may not have been built until the time of Hadrian. As a result, it has often been assumed that the *Limes* initially stood alone, simply as a chain of watchtowers, with no real military backing by forces in their immediate vicinity. This would, however, have been such appalling military practice that it is difficult to credit, for such a system would have been both pointless and suicidal.

It is assumed that the purpose of a *Limes* system was to provide an observation screen and to monitor and control movements across the frontier but, as we have already said (chapter 3), there is little point in an observation screen unless its observers can report what they see. Likewise, whilst a system lacking the manpower of a fort chain may still be able to monitor frontier movements, it would have had very little ability to control them. Such a system would, therefore, seem to fly in the face of any sensible model of Roman frontier control. The *Limes'* soldiers were not observing and monitoring for their own interest. They were part of a much wider exercise in frontier management in which the actual enforcement of control could only be exercised by response centres of sufficient power to impose their authority. This meant that from the very outset the frontier needed forts, for which the minor installations were merely eyes and ears. A system which did not contain forts would simply have turned valuable highly trained soldiers into hostages to fortune, for to leave small groups of men, unsupported, in isolated positions, in potentially hostile country, is positively to invite their destruction. In fact, however, there is a certain (admittedly limited) amount of evidence that the original plan for the *Limes* did, indeed, involve forts, albeit much smaller in scale than the later auxiliary bases. For excavations at a number of the principal stone *Limes* forts, including Saalburg, Altenstadt (Schönberger & Simon 1983) and Kapersburg (Helmke 1924) in the Wetterau, and Zugmantel (O.R.L., Abt. B, Band II, 1, Nr 8) in the Taunus mountains further west, have revealed earlier, and rather smaller, turf and timber forts which do seem to date from the earliest days of the system. Little is known of the interiors of these early forts, but their defences show sufficient uniformity to be diagnostic. They are square, rather than the more familiar playing card shaped rectangle, and their sizes fall within a range of between, roughly, 0.6 and 0.9ha.

The fact that so few of these structures have so far come to light need cause us little surprise, for we are still largely dependent on the nineteenth- and early twentieth-century excavations of the *Reichslimeskommission* for our knowledge of *Limes* forts. The commission was undertaking the massive task of studying the entire line and the techniques of the day were, anyway, better suited to dealing with stone forts than with any predecessors in less durable materials. Even today these early forts have only been found, by excavation, on sites where really large scale work has been done and it is perhaps more surprising that the commission performed as well as it did. But recent work in the Wetterau may be able, tentatively, to add two more primary forts. Firstly, a remarkable aerial photograph of Ober-Florstadt (Baatz & Herrmann 1989, 35 & Abb 18), as well as showing clear outlines of the unexcavated internal buildings and a previously unknown annexe, revealed part of the ditch of a smaller fort underlying the known *Limeskastell*. The only published drawing derived from this picture (Wagner 1986, 282) assumes that the ditch belongs to a smaller rectangular fort of about 0.74ha. But there is no evidence to support this apparently arbitrary interpretation, for the aerial photograph shows only the south side and south-west corner of the structure which may well thus be square. The writer also understands from Prof. D. Baatz that recent, and as yet unpublished, excavations at Echzell may, for the first time, have found a full auxiliary unit sized primary fort, rather than the long suspected smaller installation on this site. There is, therefore, a strong and growing possibility that more, and perhaps even all, of the *Limes* forts had such ancestors.

With this in mind, it is worth taking another look at the signalling data and, in particular, at the tactical oddities mentioned in the layout of the northern zone of the study sector. For example, the course of the northernmost part of the Wetterau loop from WP

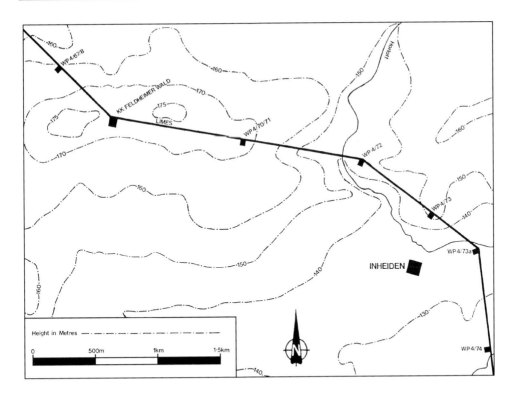

*68 The Inheiden sector*

4/47 to WP 4/64 (*see* **53 & 54**) runs almost exactly along the limit of view of the fort of Arnsburg. Indeed, for much of this run the line is so close to that limit that only the tower tops would have been visible from the fort. To have managed to find such a position for a fort, if it was built to relate to a pre-existing *Limes*, would have taken a great deal of luck, as well as superlative skill. But when we also consider the superb position of the fort, which is sited on a strong plateau, within easy reach of a water source (the River Wetter), the coincidence becomes a little too striking. Arnsburg, as currently understood, would appear to post-date the line (Kröll & Schönberger 1965), but it would be easier to believe that the process was actually the reverse with the *Limes* being laid out with reference to a pre-existing, or planned, fort on or near the Arnsburg site.

An identical situation can be found, if on a smaller scale, in the area from KK Feldheimer Wald to WP 4/70/71 to the north of the *Numeruskastell* at Inheiden (**68**). In this stretch the *Limes* runs just to the rear of the crest of a gentle ridge. Had it been actually on the crest it would have enjoyed an impressive view north into free Germany, but sited where it is it has a very limited view north. Once again the explanation seems to be that the *Limes* is here running along the exact limit of view of the fort (**69**). Indeed, again, only its tower tops would have been in sight and, such is the shape of the ridge, that, whilst the line taken by the frontier was just visible from Inheiden, the stronger ground on the crest, despite its higher elevation, was not. The fact that the line was arranged in this way, to its

*69 The view from Inheiden to KK Feldheimer Wald (1) and WP 4/70/71 (2)*

considerable tactical disadvantage may, therefore, suggest that Inheiden, like Arnsburg, was planned or already in existence in some form at the time the frontier was built, and it is worth remembering that KK Feldheimer Wald (and any preceding watchtower), which provided the strategic link between Inheiden and Arnsburg, forms part of this sector and stands on the only point visible from both.

Another superb recent aerial photograph by Braasch (1983, 74) may confirm this interpretation for Inheiden. For, as well as showing the long-known *c.*0.67ha *Numeruskastell* (O.R.L., Abt, B, Band II, 2, Nr 17) excavated in 1885 and 1910, it also shows what appear to be at least two further forts on the same site. One of these is of the primary type, being square and *c.*0.88ha in size, whilst the second is a little larger (*c.*1.2ha) and not quite square in shape (*c.*100m x 120m). The photograph also shows a number of *vicus* buildings fronting onto a road which issues from the south gate of the 0.88ha fort and appears unrelated to the known *Numeruskastell*. This apparent primary fort does, however, show signs of having stone, rather than timber gate towers and what appear to be the robber trenches of a stone headquarters building, so that a final analysis must await further excavation.

Additional evidence for primary forts elsewhere may come from the way in which a number of line installations appear to have been deliberately weakened, and the best example here is WP 4/64 to the east of Arnsburg. As we have already seen, the *Limes* in this area makes skilful use of the terrain and, as a result, usually enjoys a strong tactical position, whilst many of the minor installations occupy hilltops. A very few, however, lie to the rear of the strongest ground and this is particularly true of WP 4/64. The tower sits on a small area of roughly level ground behind the summit of one of the boldest hills in the vicinity, immediately to the north of the modern village of Bettenhausen (**53, 70A &**

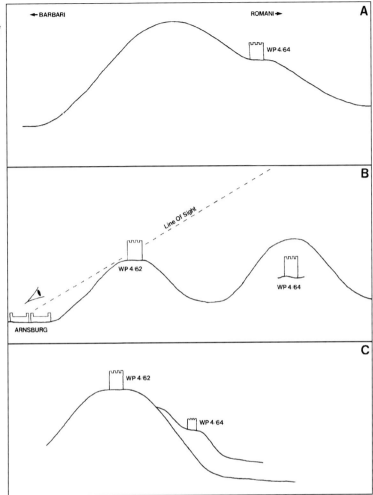

*70 The topography between Arnsburg and WP 4/64*

**71**). Yet just forward of the tower the ground rises again to form a commanding summit which would have given the tower a magnificent view north into Barbarian territory and a very strong tactical position. The fact that this opportunity was not taken requires explanation, for the tower as built, even from its full height, can see no more than a few metres out from the *Limes*, and simply looks straight into the hillside.

Once again, however, the solution may lie in the relationship between the frontier line and its nearest fort. For between WP 4/64 and Arnsburg lies a lower hill which carries WP 4/62 (**71**). WP 4/62 does stand right on the summit of its hill and is in full view of the fort, but despite its lower elevation, this hill completely blocks Arnsburg's view of the summit of WP 4/64's hill (**70B**). However, if we look at the actual view from the fort, as depicted in **70C**, we can see that WP 4/64, as sited, is just intervisible with Arnsburg around the shoulder of the hill bearing WP 4/62. In fact, the positioning is even more precise than has been shown, for clarity's sake, in the diagram. For the tower is actually on the highest point it possibly could be on the hill whilst still retaining intervisibility with Arnsburg and

*71 Telephoto view of WP 4/62 (1) and WP 4/64 (2) from Arnsburg*

would, again, only have been visible from the fort at its full height. Nevertheless, the tower as sited preserves a link with the fort both for itself and, via its capacity as a relay, for its immediate neighbours, even though the tactical cost is considerable. It seems inconceivable that a tower would be weakened in this way, unless the object was, indeed, to preserve its intervisibility with Arnsburg. Whilst we can, so far, say nothing about the remaining forts on the study sector, we may, once again, feel strongly entitled to suspect that a fort of some kind was planned, or already in existence at Arnsburg by the time the *Limes* itself was laid out. As at Inheiden, there is a possibility that such an early fort has now been discovered on the site, although remarkably this does not, as yet, seem to have been noticed. For, since my own survey was conducted, a recent book on the area (Anon, undated, 9) has published an air photograph of Arnsburg which shows two sides of what appears to be a Roman military double ditch partly underlying the known fort. For the moment this aerial feature has not been examined by excavation and so its identity cannot be regarded as proven, but Roman military installations are so distinctive in shape that the author, at least, would have few doubts.

# 5 The Upper German/Raetian border

## The study sector

The second stretch of the German *Limes* to be studied lay over 100km to the south-east in Baden-Württemberg and consisted of the 69km sector from Watch Post 9/120, north of Welzheim, to WP 12/107 near the fort of Halheim (*see* **49**, sector 2). As already mentioned, it was chosen for three main reasons. Firstly, like the Wetterau sector, it is one of the few parts of the line which is both long enough to act as a significant sample of the whole (*c.*15 per cent) and largely free of modern forestry. Secondly, although the first *c.*20km still lie, like the Wetterau, in the Roman province of Germania Superior, the bulk of the sector lies in Raetia. It thus provides a chance to look at the frontier arrangements of yet another province. Moreover, unlike the Upper German *Limes*, the frontier in Raetia eventually came to be covered by a stone wall, albeit somewhat lighter in construction than Hadrian's Wall. As it seems reasonable to assume that the start of this so-called '*Teufelsmauer*' (Devil's Wall) in the Rotenbachtal, near the fort of Schirenhof, marks the exact position of the provincial boundary, it also gives us an almost unprecedented opportunity to study the effects on a frontier of crossing such a border. This should allow us to detect any differences of approach between the two sides and, in particular, to see if the frontier remained integrated across the entire sector, or formed two separate, single province systems which happened to meet at one point.

Finally, when taken together, the two German sectors allow us to look at the *Limes*' evolution over time. One of the reasons the initial Wetterau sector was chosen was the fact that it was one of the earliest parts of the system and an area in which the frontier's entire development took place on the same line. The latter point is significant, because as this sector now seems to have been designed to facilitate direct signalling, we can be sure that this was an important consideration from the outset and not something for which the need only became apparent after operational experience. It does not, however, prove that signalling remained a priority. If security was later relaxed, or procedures changed so that signalling was neglected in favour of other means of communication, this might leave no sign in the archaeological record simply because, with the line remaining constant, the traces of the original policy would remain fossilised, as it were, in its very fabric. This may seem a slightly pedantic point, but it should be remembered that a substantial number of Hadrian's Wall's turrets were abandoned soon after the system's reoccupation in the aftermath of the abandonment of the Antonine Wall in the mid-second century. This must reflect a change in the Wall's operating procedures. This second study sector, however,

*72 The start of the Teufelsmauer on the west side of the Rotenbachtal*

allows us a look at the same frontier at the other end of its building history at least a generation later in the AD 150s, and any significant changes in operational priorities over that period should be reflected in its design.

This second study area's layout and topography is also worth comparing with the Wetterau sector. It will be remembered that the latter broke down into two zones. Both contained forts set at reasonably regular 6-7km intervals, with the line installations sited so as to be intervisible with their neighbours, rather than to a regular spacing pattern. But, in the southern zone, the forts lay close to the line, often in valley bottoms and the frontier itself followed a straight course taking no tactical account of the terrain. In the north, the forts were built well to the rear, often in stronger positions and with the frontier itself following a freer course so as to gain the maximum tactical advantage from the ground. The northern zone also enjoyed an almost perfect direct signalling system, whilst the southern zone tended rather more towards a linear system. The present sector also shows these two layout patterns. The same basic elements (forts, towers and *Kleinkastelle*) are still present, although the fort intervals tend to be longer and less regular (ranging from 6km (Lorch to Schirenhof) to 13km (Buch to Halheim)). But, whilst the bulk of the sector (*Limes* Stretch 12[1]) is laid out like the northern Wetterau zone, with the forts set well back and the line making sound tactical use of the terrain, the first *c.*8km forms part of *Limes* Stretch 9, which, with Stretch 8, runs almost perfectly straight, with its forts set right behind the line, for *c.*80km until only 19km south of the River Main.

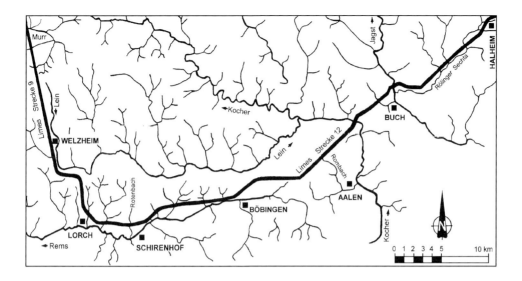

*73 The river valleys of the* Limes *study sector*

Geographically (**73**), the sector begins by running along the western side of the Lein valley. It then follows the northern crest of the Rems valley (except for a brief excursion down to the valley floor, west of Unterböbingen), until just before Aalen, whereupon it follows a ring of low hills to the north, before crossing the Kocher and Jagst near the fort of Buch and gaining the valley of the Röhlinger Sechta, which it follows most of the way to Halheim. In all, the 69km sector contains seven forts (Welzheim, Lorch, Schirenhof, Böbingen, Aalen, Buch and Halheim) and current maps show 125 line installations, including four *Kleinkastelle* and the Dalkingen *Limes* gate.

## The signalling system

Since the bulk of the study sector closely resembles the northern Wetterau zone in layout, one might also expect its signalling arrangements to be similar (assuming that the Romans were still giving signalling such a high priority by this date) and this does appear to be the case. The forts have been carefully sited to enjoy a good view of the line, which (as on both Hadrian's Wall and the northern Wetterau zone) often runs along their exact skyline. The line sites themselves are almost always sited so as to enjoy a good view back from the *Limes*, even though this frequently meant their having little or no view forward (e.g. WP 12/13, 12/17, 12/42 and 12/83). Indeed, in view of the often difficult terrain through which it passes, the frontier has been elegantly laid out to facilitate signalling, for the entire sector (including even the straight southern end of *Limes* Stretch 9) comes close to a true direct system (*see* **78**) and was obviously designed as such. For example, the sectors around Welzheim, Böbingen and Buch (**75**) are almost textbook examples, with almost every single line installation enjoying a direct view to their fort. In the first case, this seems

*74 The Dalkingen* Limes *gate*

almost accidental, because Stretch 9 is so different from Stretch 12, and although Welzheim itself may have a perfect view of its surroundings, most of this long straight sector resembles the southern Wetterau zone. Böbingen and Buch, on the other hand, seem to have been carefully sited to promote signalling. Böbingen was built on a small plateau, part way up the south side of the Rems valley, to enhance its view of the frontier line on the north side, whilst Buch stands on a prominent high point intervisible with a long stretch of frontier, which has been skillfully looped around it (**76**).

Elsewhere, however, the terrain made such perfection impossible. At Aalen, for example, a complex series of hills and stream valleys ruled out a similar direct system unless the fort was built so far up the southern side of the Rombach valley that it would have caused tactical problems of its own by building a serious delay into the garrison's potential response time to emergencies. Instead, the Romans simply ran the line along a series of ridges to the north, on the shortest route to Buch and set the fort itself on a high point, just north of the river from which much, but not all, of the line is in view. This is obviously a compromise solution, but it has been implemented with skill and the fort still enjoys simple one-stage relay links with its neighbours (Böbingen and Buch) via WP 12/55 and 12/71, whilst only six of the 17 line installations between these points would need relays for their signals to reach the fort. Moreover, many of the line sites which appear on maps of this sector are in fact only conjectural. Of the sites actually known to exist, only WP 12/66 would need a relay, whilst some of the theoretical sites, notably WP 12/63 and 69, have been allocated rather unlikely positions in narrow valley bottoms with almost no view in any direction.

75 *Telephoto view of the* Limes *from Buch fort with a modern reconstruction of WP 12/77 (arrowed)*

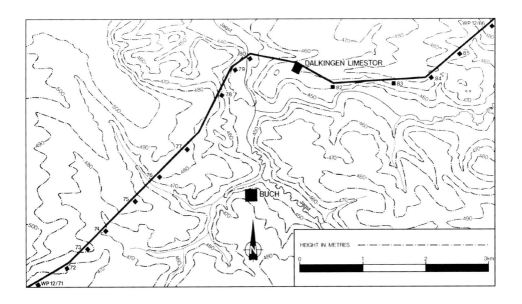

76 *The* Limes *around the fort of Buch*

Schirenhof is rather more like Böbingen. The winding Rems valley is almost a gorge at this point and the fort has been built on a plateau some 50m above the valley floor, on the south side of the river, to improve its view of the *Limes*. This succeeds in putting the fort in visual touch with the line installations to its north and immediate west, but its view east remains obscured by a still higher ridge. As a result, the fort can see almost none of line sites to its east and needs a double relay (via WPs 12/30 and 12/34) to communicate with Böbingen. There would in fact have been more than enough room for a fort on the top of this eastern ridge, and the far better view thus obtained would have allowed a one relay signalling link with Böbingen (via WP 12/34) and brought more line installations into sight. But in other ways the ridge would not have been a good fort site. Its top, which is the only viable building area, stands 120m above the Rems. Its steep sides would have greatly impaired the garrison's mobility, again making it harder to rush to the aid of the *Limes* in a crisis, as well as hindering more mundane tasks such as provisioning and obtaining water. So, again, the Romans may have compromised. The signalling system still works with the fort as built and they may simply have traded a potential improvement for convenience in other areas. There may even have been a watchtower on the ridge top to act as an additional eye, although no evidence has, so far, come to light. Whatever the case, the signalling restraints imposed by the fort's actual position, coupled to the topographical complexity of the *Limes* line itself, which crosses a number of deep stream valleys in the area, may help to explain an unusual concentration of *Kleinkastelle* in the sector. Although, in the case of KK's Kleindeinbach and Freimühle, which stand on opposite sides of the Rotenbachtal, the Upper German-Raetian border may also be a explanatory factor.

It is towards the western end of the study sector, however, that we have the best demonstration of the skill with which Roman frontier designers could exploit difficult terrain to facilitate signalling. One of the most obvious questions with the layout of the study sector is: why does the long straight of Stretches 8 and 9 end where it does at the start of Stretch 12? Beyond this point, the *Limes* has to transfer from one topographical feature, the Lein Valley, to the Rems Valley, and if the line had simply continued on straight, it would have crossed a series of ridges to the east of the Walkersbach before reaching the Rems slightly downstream of the fort of Lorch (**77**). Instead, it swings east at WP 12/1, then south at WP 12/5, to follow the ridge between two streams known as the Aimersbach and Götzenbach, before finally turning eastwards again at WP 12/11 to cross the Götzenbach and reach the Rems Valley just upstream of Lorch at WP 12/14.

The equally obvious explanation is that the direct route would have been tactically less appropriate and the complex terrain would have made communications much more difficult. There is no easy route from the Lein to the Rems, but by utilising the ridge on which WP 12/6-11 stand, the Romans placed the line on the most consistent run of high ground available, which puts the frontier towers on far better observation positions and greatly improves the signalling situation. It is true that, even here, none of the ridge top towers can see Lorch, which is not intervisible with anything north of WP 12/12. This situation though could not have been significantly improved unless the fort had been sited well above river level to the south of the Rems. That is, of course, exactly what was done at Schirenhof and Böbingen but, as at Aalen, it would have been far more difficult here,

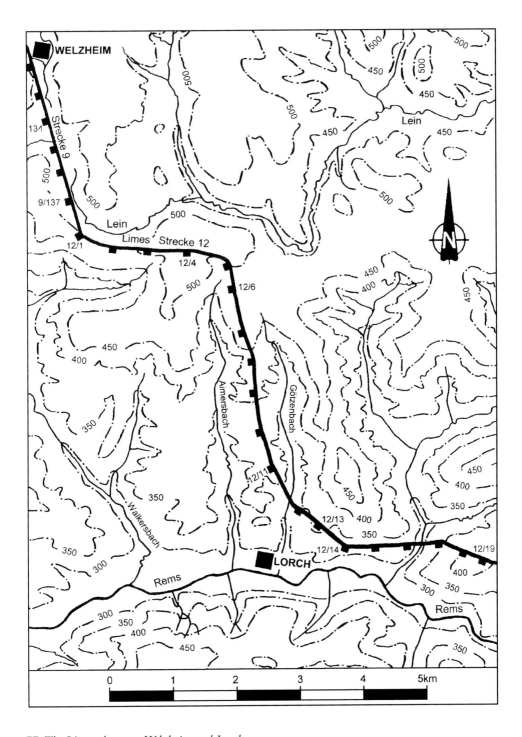

77 *The* Limes *between Welzheim and Lorch*

because there is no convenient plateau on the steep south slope. This means that the fort could only have been built away from the valley bottom by being moved right up to its southern crest, 170m above the Rems, from where it would have been hard to provide close support for the frontier line and control of the Rems valley route ways. Instead, therefore, the fort has been placed down in the valley bottom, close to water and supply routes, on a site north of the river which gave unobstructed access to the *Limes*. This might at first sight appear to be rather too much of a compromise, but, unlike Schirenhof and Böbingen, where there was little alternative but to site the forts to the south of the Rems, Lorch offered other possibilities. The *Limes* swings to cross the Götzenbach well upstream of its confluence with the Rems. But instead of then turning onto what might seem the most obvious line, a direct route to the hill bearing WP 12/19 (**77**), it deviates south towards Kloster Lorch. This has two important consequences. Firstly, it puts WP 12/13 on the top of a sub-ridge from where it can see, and so link, Lorch and every line installation from WP 12/3 to 12/11. The site thus becomes a vital relay, perhaps explaining its much larger than usual size (ORL Abt A, Band VI, 34f and Tafel 3). As WP 12/3 can see Welzheim, the site also allows the two forts to be linked via just two relays, a considerable achievement in such difficult country. The second, almost as impressive, effect is to put WP 12/14 at Kloster Lorch, on what is the northernmost point in the vicinity which can still see Lorch from the height of a Roman tower. This allows it to link the fort with WP 12/15-17, giving all of the area's line sites one-stage relays to Lorch.

So far, within the limits imposed by the ground, the system has been neatly and skilfully laid out, but there are two small sectors which do not seem to fit the overall pattern. The first is the stretch between WP 12/90 and 12/98 (**78**). The line here apparently runs along the bottom of the Röhlinger Sechta Valley putting much of it out of sight of the well-sited fort of Halheim, forcing all nine towers to use WP 12/101 as a relay to the fort. This is the longest run of blind sites anywhere on either of the two *Limes* study sectors, affecting two more towers even than the ridge north of Lorch. Yet at Lorch, we were dealing with extremely difficult terrain, whereas this situation could have been prevented simply by running the line a little to either the north or south of the valley. It should be said, however, that the very course of the *Limes* in this area is somewhat uncertain, so this situation may prove to be illusory. At least one tower has been claimed to lie *c.*400m south of the currently mapped line (see Appendix 2, WP 12/98) on a position that would have been able to see the fort.

The second unusual area has already been mentioned, the *Limes'* curious detour down to the Rems, to the west of Böbingen. Throughout most of the Rems Valley sector the line is configured like Hadrian's Wall and the northern Wetterau zone in that it runs along the northern limit of the forts' fields of view. In this particular area, this would have involved continuing the line between WP 12/54 and 12/46 (**78**) further west and then following a route through the modern villages of Iggingen and Herlikofen to WP 12/34. This course would have given the line an excellent view to the north, as well as leaving every watch post in full view of Böbingen. But instead, a 10 installation (9km) stretch has been run along the steep valley side, to the south of that ideal line. The 1.5km stretch from WP 12/38 to 12/41 is actually down on the valley floor.[2] Interestingly, even on this line, the frontier installations all retain visual contact with the fort, but the deviation is otherwise

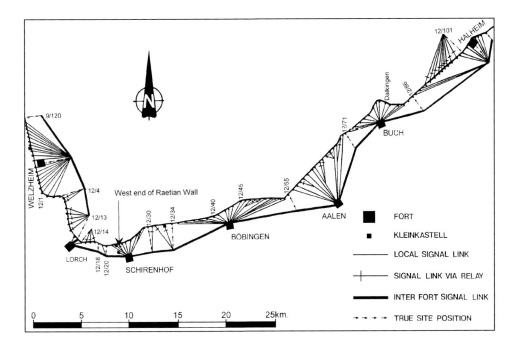

*78 The signalling system of the southern* Limes *study sector using all mapped installations*

baffling. It is a tactical absurdity, which forces the line across far more difficult terrain. It surrenders much of the watch posts' surveillance capability to the north and abandons an, albeit small, part of the Rems valley bottom, which must have been important as a communications artery. There is no obvious military justification. The only rational explanation to date has been that recently put forward by Hodgson (1997, 63) who has suggested that, as the frontier to the east of this area may have been built slightly before that to the west, the line may originally have ended beside the Rems, much as Stretch 5 rests on the Main. If so, it may be relevant that the frontier reaches the river at the furthest point downstream still visible from Böbingen and certainly, although the Rems is a much smaller river than the Main, the author has no better analysis to offer. It is even possible that the line may eventually prove to have been re-routed onto a more northerly line at this point, once the western part of the sector was constructed. For a long straight surface feature has long been known to run through Iggingen and Herlikofen on what would have been the ideal course, which is strongly reminiscent of a Roman road.

We can now look again at the sector as a whole, but this is not quite as simple as it might appear, because of the way in which the *Limes* has been studied in the past. It is undeniable that the sheer scale of the *Reichslimeskommission*'s achievement, in producing its huge multi-volume report on the entire frontier (the ORL), is all but unparalleled in the history of archaeology. But, although a great deal of work has been done since, in and around the forts, there has been remarkably little subsequent interest in the line itself, and modern maps of the frontier tend largely to repeat those of the ORL. What is easily forgotten, however, although the *Limeskommission* freely admitted it, is that disappointingly few of the line sites are categorically known to exist. A high proportion of those on the ORL maps were simply invented, either because a particular spot appeared advantageous, or to fill up a gap in the spacing pattern. No doubt many of these sites do in fact exist, on or near to their mapped positions, and there are a number of other unexcavated towers for which there is, at least, some evidence (see Appendix 2). This may take the form of folklore, old records, stray finds, or the memories of people alive when the commission was active, and it is sometimes fairly convincing. But it often consists of no more than stones or mortar being ploughed up in a particular place, which could come from almost anything, and is particularly weak in an area strewn with the wreckage of the Teufelsmauer. We must thus face the fact that of the 125 mapped towers on the study sector, only 43 (34 per cent) are known with absolute certainty, if with some evidence for 22 more. This means that we need to present two different signalling models: the first to include the full set of mapped installations, the second restricted to the known sites. Neither is likely to represent the whole truth because, although there must once have been far more sites than the relatively few known examples, some of the assumed sites will be either non-existent or located far enough away from their mapped positions to make a material difference. But this is the best that can be done for the moment and we should at least be able to determine the general pattern even if details are wrong.

To look at the full corpus first (**78**), 92 towers (74 per cent) can communicate directly with a fort, whilst the remaining 33 (26 per cent) can all have their signals passed to a fort via simple one-stage relays. Inter-fort communications are also relatively straightforward and the forts seem to have clear-cut areas of responsibility. None of the forts are directly intervisible but, of the six inter-fort links on the sector, three can be accomplished by single-stage relays (Böbingen to Aalen, Aalen to Buch, and Buch to Halheim), whilst the remainder require relaying via two other sites. It is also noteworthy that here, as on other frontiers, the relays for both inter-fort and line installation signals are always on the same side of the receiving fort as the site they are serving. Thus although the fort can no longer see the source of a relayed signal, it will still know which direction the signal is coming from. The inter-fort system does, though, show one small difference from the northern Wetterau zone, because here there are fewer indications that the inter-fort relays have been singled out or protected in any way. In the Wetterau, *Kleinkastelle* were used in this role, perhaps as what would now be called 'hardened installations', to ensure that communications could survive some degree of enemy attack. But, in this southern stretch, the relay sites are all ordinary towers, albeit some, such as WP 12/13, are rather larger than normal. Indeed, to date, only four *Kleinkastelle* are known on the sector, compared to 14 on the slightly shorter Wetterau study area. Finally, and most importantly, despite the *Kleinkastell* concentration in its immediate vicinity, there is no sign whatever of a significant change of approach as the signalling system crosses the Upper German-Raetian border. In fact Schirenhof's signalling sector seems to span parts of both provinces and, although our knowledge of the first few kilometres of the Upper German side is poor, the two provincial frontiers appear to have been well integrated to form a single unified whole. Indeed, the very existence of a provincial boundary could not be inferred from the signalling data alone, and it seems that military signalling could cut across administrative boundaries.

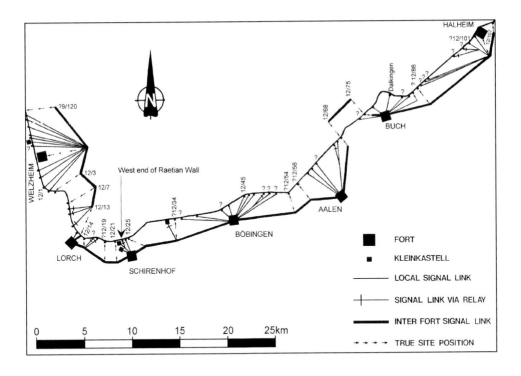

79 *The signalling system of the southern* Limes *study sector using known and likely installations only*

Building a signals model with only the known installations is rather more difficult. Indeed, it is simply impossible using just the 43 excavated watch posts. But if we add in the 22 sites for which some evidence exists, we arrive at the pattern shown in **79**. Interestingly, once the data has been stripped down in this way, we are left (perhaps not surprisingly) with a more truly direct signalling system. For, of the 65 remaining sites, all but 12 (18.5 per cent) have a clear view to a fort, as opposed to 26 per cent with the full ORL catalogue. The situation is even better with the excavated towers, where all except seven (16 per cent) out of 43 are intervisible with a fort. It is also noteworthy that of the two unusual sectors mentioned above, none of the Rems valley bottom sites (WP 12/38-40) are firmly known to exist, whilst of the nine in the Röhlinger Sechta Valley (WP 12/90-98), only WP 12/96 is known. Inter-fort communications, however, although still possible, do suffer markedly with the reduced data set. Halheim and Buch can still be linked by the same one-stage relay via WP 12/86, but the connections between Aalen and Buch, and Böbingen and Aalen now need two-stage relays via WP 12/68 and 76, and 12/54 and 56 respectively. Schirenhof and Böbingen are still linked by a double relay, this time via WP 12/25 and 34, but the links from Welzheim to Lorch and Lorch to Schirenhof now need triple relays via WP 12/3, 7 and 13, and 12/14, 19 and 21 respectively. It should however be stressed that this situation should improve as more towers are discovered.

## *Limes* Stretch 8/9 v Stretch 12

Once again, on this study sector, we appear to have found the Romans going to considerable trouble to equip a frontier with an efficient direct signalling system, despite topographical difficulties and a number of compromises dictated by other operational requirements. But, as in the Wetterau, there are complications. Even in the westernmost part of the study sector we find the *Limes* reverting to a tactically illogical straight course and although, in the area around Welzheim, this still leaves direct signalling possible, other parts of the long 80km straight of Stretches 8 and 9 are not so fortunate. But there is an important difference in the terrain between Stretch 8/9 and Stretch 12, or at least in the line's relationship to it, which raises a fascinating possibility that might also have relevance to the southern Wetterau zone. For there are signs emerging that there may be not one, but two recurring frontier designs. The first runs the line essentially parallel to the principle landscape features (river valleys, ridges, coast lines etc.) and might be called a 'terrain-following' system. These tend to have their forts set back from the line for a better view along these features and have direct or near direct signalling systems. The second type might be called 'terrain-crossing' systems as the line runs roughly at right angles to the topography, often running far straighter and taking far less notice of tactical possibilities. These tend more towards linear signalling and their forts are usually much closer to the line, as there is less to be gained from setting them back. Their forts are also frequently set down in river valleys, closer to water and transportation corridors, often guarding the easiest routes into and out of the Roman Empire.

This dichotomy exists in both the present study sector, with the differences between Stretches 9 and 12, and in the Wetterau, where the southern zone is largely terrain-crossing and the northern zone terrain-following. It would seem, in fact, that both designs may be striving towards direct signalling. As the towers of a terrain-crossing system are often on higher ground than their nearest fort, a high proportion are still often intervisible with it, despite the apparent lack of interest in exploiting the ground. Nevertheless, signalling is easier on a terrain-following system since, if the forts are set back from the principle surface features, they are less easily cut off by undulations within them. Terrain-crossing systems, on the other hand, face the problem that there will often be more than one ridge or valley between two forts, and will thus almost inevitably contain some linear signalling components. Perhaps for this reason, terrain parallel systems seem to be more common and were probably the preferred option. For example, Hadrian's Wall follows four main east-west running features, the Whin Sill ridge and the rivers Tyne, Irthing and Eden. The Antonine Wall follows the Forth and Kelvin valleys. The Gask frontier follows Strathallan and the Gask Ridge, and the Cumberland Coast defences are terrain-following by definition. Only where nothing else was possible do the Romans seem to have adopted the terrain-crossing approach, and in the case of *Limes* Stretches 8 and 9 nothing else would have been possible without running the frontier very much further to the north.

In addition to these two basic layout types, there are also hybrid sectors which combine elements of both. For example, the initial design of Hadrian's Wall used a series of pre-existing rearward forts on the Stanegate road and was a true terrain-following system. But these forts were mostly later abandoned for new forts on the line of the Wall itself, and the Antonine Wall was built in this Wall fort configuration from the start. In both cases the line forts were constructed in highly visible positions, usually on hilltops, rather than the valley bottoms used by terrain-crossing sectors in Germany, but their signalling capabilities still suffered as a result. Another example might be the area around Welzheim because, although still part of the long straight towards the Main, this stretch actually runs parallel to a topographical feature, the Lein valley, rather than across it. If so, it could be argued that the frontier reverted to a terrain-following configuration at WP 9/120, rather than 12/1, in which case it becomes even less surprising that it follows its present line across to the Rems, rather than taking the more direct route mentioned above. This leaves the position of the fort, close to the *Limes*, as a hybrid element, but as Welzheim can still see every line installation in its vicinity, there may simply have been no advantage in siting it further away and its proximity would have improved its response time. The fort does, though, show one other anomaly for which there is no obvious signalling explanation. For there are actually two forts on the site to house two different units simultaneously and, uniquely, the so-called Ostkastell was built outside rather than inside the line.

The hybrids do, of course, raise one final question, the relative merits of siting forts on or back from the line. Both the original design of Hadrian's Wall and the terrain-following parts of the *Limes* frequently ran the line along the skyline as seen from the forts. In other words the line lay as far from the forts as it possibly could be, if signalling links were to be preserved. Indeed so precisely has this been done that the frontier installations are frequently only intervisible with the forts from their full original heights. This might suggest that the Romans preferred to keep a distance between the forts and the line and, so long as this did not become excessive, there were certainly advantages in doing so. We have already seen that rearward forts will often have a better view of the frontier, and in the case of sites such as Schirenhof, which lies on the opposite side of a valley, they might even have gained a view over intervening forest. It would also be easier for a fort garrison to intercept any raiders who actually managed to penetrate the frontier if it was operating from a base in the rear and not simply having to give chase. Moreover, as most forts were supervising between 6-12km of frontier, being sited a little behind the line would have made surprisingly little difference to their response time in sending help to the bulk of that sector, especially in view of the more efficient signalling system the separation permitted. Lastly, as the forts on any frontier are usually on or near the main communication routes, running the frontier well to the front might help both to keep these routes secure and to increase the garrisons' interception capacity, by enhancing their lateral mobility. Against this, putting a fort on the frontier gives it an immediate visible presence to enhance its deterrent value (although this would diminish towards the limits of a fort's area of responsibility). It might also make it easier for the Romans to pass through the line, to project force beyond their own territory, especially on systems like the two British Walls, which had fort gates through the running barrier.

Which location option was better would no doubt vary with circumstances but, as it is not hard to point to situations where it would have still been advantageous for a terrain-crossing system to set its forts back from the line, the fact that this was so rarely done requires comment. A prime example would again be Marköbel in the southern Wetterau zone. As we saw in chapter 4, this site was built close behind the *Limes*. Yet had it been set just a few hundred metres further back, it would have been able to see past a hill to five currently blind *Limes* sites and so dramatically improve its sector's communications. The author has suggested that this opportunity may have been ignored because of heavy tree cover in the area, which would have forced the frontier to follow a narrow, straight, cleared corridor, along which signals could have been passed. If so, the presence of forest might also explain the fort positions of some of the other terrain-crossing sectors in Germany. It may even offer another reason why Welzheim, on a terrain-following part of the line, should, alone amongst all of the forts on the southern study sector, be sited so close to the line. For, like Marköbel, the line is here straight and if it had been forested in Roman times signals could only have been passed to the fort had it been in line with a linear clearing along the frontier.

## Notes

1   The *Limes* is divided into 15 so-called 'Stretches', but these are modern divisions and do not have any ancient significance. They originated in the lengths of line parceled out to the various officials of the *Reichslimeskommission* in the late nineteenth century and now serve as navigational references.
2   ORL Abt A, Band VI, Karte 1 shows the line actually crossing the river, although this is both unproven and unlikely.

# 6 Conclusion

This book set out to address two basic issues. The first, which is more local and technical in nature, was simply to find out whether Roman frontiers could have been equipped with comprehensive signalling systems and, if so, to discover how they worked, what technology they had available, how effective this was, and how their requirements might have influenced the overall design of the defences. The second, and more wide-ranging, was to look at several frontiers and attempt to see whether each was a unique independent design, or whether they had enough features in common to raise the possibility that most, or even all, Roman linear land frontiers might be based on some form of Empire-wide 'blueprint' or principle.

So far as the first is concerned, it is to be hoped that the question has now been answered and that this book has demonstrated that all of the frontiers studied were capable of operating signalling systems using workable techniques to which all of their installations could be connected. It has, of course, been freely admitted throughout that it is almost impossible to then go on and prove that such systems were ever in use. Given the limitations of archaeology and the absence of written accounts it can only be shown that they could have been. But numerous examples have been quoted here where the, apparently irrational, positioning of frontier sectors and/or installations would only seem to make sense if they had been intended to facilitate communications. When taken together, these do seem to make a highly persuasive case that signalling was practised on Roman frontiers and was, indeed, assigned such a high priority that other aspects of frontier design could be compromised to enhance it. The balance of probabilities, therefore, is that highly effective signalling systems did exist on these frontiers and that they did have a significant influence on the details of frontier design.

As to the second issue, one cannot deny the many differences between individual Roman frontiers and there was, no doubt, considerable local control over their initial construction and layout. This is hardly surprising, for every frontier would have needed to respond to its own geographic, military, political and resource circumstances and these local factors would have continued to influence their subsequent evolution. Nevertheless, there are strong common elements running through all of the frontiers studied and one of the strongest of these is the tendency to strive towards what I have called 'direct' signalling systems in which every minor installation has a direct visual link to a fort. The Stanegate phase of Hadrian's Hall may be the only near-perfect example of such a system yet found, but we have seen signs that a great deal of effort was made elsewhere to get close to this maximally efficient arrangement. This may not yet, by itself, be quite enough to prove either way whether all Roman frontiers could have been based on a single central design, and the Stanegate is currently unique in having its own set of (largely rearward)

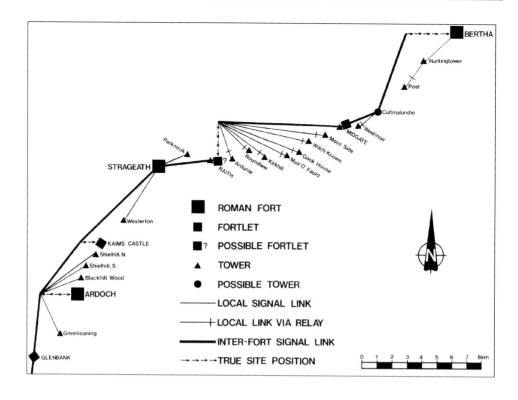

*80 The signalling system of the Gask frontier*

relay towers, which made a major contribution to its signalling potential. But it has, at least, drawn attention to a suggestive common thread and made the original question more legitimate to ask. Moreover, what are probably similar arrangements are now emerging on other frontiers, notably the Dacian *Limes* in Romania (Gudea 1997), the Antonine Wall in Britain (Woolliscroft 1996), and even on Rome's very earliest fortified land frontier: the Gask system in Scotland (Woolliscroft 1993). For the moment, then, we can at least claim that nothing has been found to discredit the idea. Nevertheless, a great deal more work remains to be done. In particular, the present work has dealt almost exclusively with the frontiers of northern Europe, mainly for logistical reasons and because these are currently the only systems that are well enough known for a signalling survey to be possible. But even here, the research to date has been little more than a reconnaissance and additional studies are continuing, whilst outside Europe Prof. M. Gichon has informed the author that he has found signs of a similar system on the frontiers of Roman Judea.

Elsewhere in the Empire, work of a more basic nature is required, simply to find the installations and, on occasions, even the line of the frontiers. It seems probable that, if there are to be fundamental breaks from the patterns my own work has revealed, then these will occur on the desert frontiers. For in these areas both hostile and peaceful movement is largely restricted to routes with available water and there is rather less need for the all-inclusive linear defences of the damper, more temperate north, where travel is less restricted. Unfortunately, work on Rome's vast desert and semi-desert frontiers has always been limited by funding restraints and by a shortage of local scholars interested in the Roman period. Nevertheless, there has long been a trickle of information from these areas which has been steadily building in recent years, and it is to be hoped that this excellent work will continue to develop. In particular, we are seeing a much-needed resurgence of aerial photography in a number of countries in North Africa and the Middle East where military tensions and an often understandable culture of secrecy previously made it difficult to continue the dramatic harvest glimpsed all too briefly in the early days of aviation. Given the political will, archaeologists and even the air forces of these countries can make a significant contribution relatively cheaply, and hopefully this trend will spread. Work in the temperate lands must also continue. Even the better-known systems of Britain and Germany continue to produce surprises. The demise of the former Eastern Bloc and the increasing openness of countries such as Romania (where a remarkable amount of work has been done) should, hopefully, present further opportunities for new discoveries. Perhaps more importantly, there should also be continued growth in the ability of archaeologists across national frontiers, to share and discuss new ideas.

# Appendix 1
## References to signalling in ancient writers

## Fire signals, beacons and beacon chains

**1.** Homer *Iliad* XVIII, 207:
Smoke goes up from a distant harried island, where men have fought a terrible battle from their city walls all day. As soon as the sun has set, a line of beacons blazes up into the sky to warn the surrounding islanders and brings them in ships to the rescue.

**2.** Aeschylus *Agamemnon* (Fig. 1) lines 7-9:
Watchman: Now I watch for a new star, the promised beacon fire, the signal bringing news from Troy of Victory.

**3.** Aeschylus *Agamemnon* lines 20-9:
Let fire lighten the dark with good news. Ah, the beacon glows. The blessed beacon, turning night into glorious day. The Queen must get up at once and welcome the fire with welcoming words and a cry of victory, for the beacon shows that Troy is ours.

**4.** Aeschylus *Agamemnon* lines 278-316 (Translation provided by Dr A.G. Keen):
CHORUS: Tell us, when was Troy taken?
CLYTEMNESTRA: Tonight.
CHORUS: What messenger could rush here that fast?
CLYTEMNESTRA: Hephaistos sent out a clear torch from Ida; beacon sent beacon hither from the courier flame. Ida sent to the crag of Hermes on Lemnos; third the heights of Zeus on Athos received the great torch from the island. The might of the travelling beacon-light rising above the sea so as to skim it, for the pleasure . . . the pine-wood torch beaming gold like some sun transmitted the message to the lookout-places of Makiston. The lookout, neither delaying nor senselessly conquered by sleep, did not disregard his share of the message, and the light, far from the beacon, came and gave a signal to the guards on Messapion, on the stream of the Euripos. They kindled a light in turn, and transmitted the message onwards, kindling with fire the heap of ancient heather. The mighty beacon-light, not yet darkened, leapt over the plain of the Asopos, after the manner of the bright moon, and gathered together another succession of the missive fire on the crag of Kithairon. The far-sent light did not renounce its duty, burning more than those spoken of. The light looked over the sea of Gorgopis, and arriving on Aigiplankton roused

the lookouts not to give up the ordinance of the fire. They sent a great beard of flame that they lit up with bounteous strength, and blazed onwards to cross the headland looking over the Saronic strait. Then it fell and reached the heights of Arachnaios, the lookout-posts near the city. And now this light fathered by the fire of Ida falls on to this house of Atreios. That, Gentlemen, was the race my signallers completed, each one faithfully doing his duty in turn. And each doing as well as the others. This is my proof sirs, a message sent to me by Agamemnon from Troy.

**5.**    Pausanias *Guide to Greece* II, 25.2:
It was to here (Lyrkeia) that Lynkeus made his legendary escape, alone of 50 brothers, and built a beacon as he promised Hypermnestra he would, as soon as he was safely away from her father. The story is that she also lit one, on Larisa, clearly to show that she was safe as well. So the Argives have an annual beacon festival.

**6.**    Herodotus *The Histories* VII, 183 (Persian War {Greek naval defeat at Sciathos} 480 BC):
The news of what had happened was sent to the Greeks at Artemisium from Sciathos by beacon.

**7.**    Herodotus IX, 3 (Persian War, 480 BC):
Mardonius had his heart set on retaking Athens, partly, no doubt, through stubbornness and partly because he planned to signal his taking of the town to the king at Sardis by means of a beacon chain through the islands.[1]

**8.**    Thucydides *The Peloponnesian War* II, 94 (429 BC):
Beacons were lit (on Salamis, relayed via Piraeus) to alert Athens that the enemy were attacking, but the inhabitants of the city thought they meant that that the enemy had entered Piraeus, causing a panic equal to any during the war.

**9.**    Thucydides *The Peloponnesian War* IV, 42 (Athenian naval operations, 425 BC):
The Athenians sailed at night and escaped detection. The Corinthians were alerted to this by beacon and arrived quickly to oppose them.

**10.**    Thucydides *The Peloponnesian War* IV, 111 (attack on Torone, 424 BC):
Brasidas moved the rest of his army forward slightly and halted. He sent 100 peltasts forward, so that when a gate was opened and the prearranged signals were sent they should charge in first. Their confederates inside Torone had been plotting with the group that had already entered . . . They then lit the prearranged fire and let in the remaining peltasts.

**11.**    Thucydides *The Peloponnesian War* VIII, 102 (411 BC):
The Athenians, with 18 ships, were at Sestos. They realised that the Peloponnesians were sailing in when told by fire signals and by seeing that numerous fires were suddenly appearing on the enemy held shore.

**12.** Aineias Tacticus 10. 25-6 (translation by kind permission of Prof. D.J. Whitehead): Something else which must be prohibited (for guards) is going with lanterns or other night lights. This is because it has been known for individuals, finding themselves utterly thwarted in their wish to start a revolution or to intrigue with the enemy, to have the idea of taking lights, torches or lanterns to their guard posts . . . they have then used these lights not for their ostensible purpose, to see to go to bed by, but to make a prearranged signal.

**13.** Aristotle *De Mundo* 398a (describing fourth-century BC Persia): So well organised was the system of signal beacons, which were ready to blaze in relays from the very frontiers of the Empire to Susa and Ecbatana, that the King came to know everything that was happening in Asia within the day.

**14.** Diodorus Siculus 19, 57, 5 (315 BC): Antigonus set up a system of beacons and messengers at intervals throughout the part of Asia he ruled. He expected these to keep him quickly abreast of affairs.

**15.** Polybius *The Histories* I, 19 (first Punic War, Heracleia, Sicily, 262 BC): After this engagement (a cavalry skirmish) Hanno took over and camped on the hill called Torus, just over a mile from the enemy. The two sides kept to these positions for two months without trying for anything more decisive than daily skirmishes. But all the time Hannibal (Gisgo, besieged *c*.20 miles away in Agrigentum) was sending fire signals and messages to remind his colleague that the inhabitants could no longer resist the famine, and that hunger was driving ever more of his men to desert to the enemy.

**16.** Polybius *The Histories* VIII, 28-9 (second Punic War, Siege of Tarentum 212 BC): The agreement between the young Terentines and Hannibal was that Hannibal was to reach the city from the east so as to approach at the area which faces inland. He was to advance on the Temenid gate, and light a fire there at the place which some call the tomb of Hyacinthus and others the tomb of Apollo. Once Tragiscus saw this, he was to light a fire from inside the walls in response. Once these signals had been exchanged, Hannibal was to extinguish his and slowly advance on the gate . . . After a time Hannibal's force approached and gave the scheduled signal. As soon as they saw the fire Nicon, Tragiscus and their associates, with their courage restored, lit their own signal in response. Then as soon as Hannibal's signal was out, they ran to the gate tower as fast as they could . . . to ambush and kill the guards.

**17.** Appian *Spanish Wars* 6, 15. 90-2 (siege of Numantia 133 BC): After setting seven forts round the city, Scipio started the siege, writing to each of the allied tribes, to tell them what troops he wanted them to send. When they arrived he split them into a number of groups and subdivided his own army. He then named a commander for each division and told them to encircle the city with a ditch and palisade. Numantia was 24 stades in circumference and the siege works were twice this size. The whole length was portioned out between the various divisions, with orders that if the enemy should attack them anywhere they should signal to him by raising a red banner on a long spear in daytime or by a fire at night, so that he and Maximus could rush to help anyone who needed it . . . He built towers along the whole of this wall at 100ft intervals. When all was ready . . . he posted messengers at frequent intervals along the whole wall to pass messages to one another by day and night to tell him what was happening. His orders to each tower were that in an emergency the one that was attacked first should signal and when the others saw this they should do likewise so that he would hear that there was trouble quickly via the signal and then be informed of the details afterwards by messenger . . . Every man was to take up his action station whenever any signal of an attack was made.

**18.** Appian *The Civil Wars* I, 6. 51 (Social War, 89 BC):
Sulla advanced quickly on Bovanum, where the rebel council was held. The city had three citadels and whilst the inhabitants were watching him carefully from one of them, Sulla ordered a detachment to take whichever of the other two they could and then send a smoke signal. When the smoke was seen he attacked and took the city after a hard three-hour fight.

**19.** Cicero *The Verrine Orations* II, 5. 35 (Translation by Dr B Hoffmann) (Negligence allows pirates to burn a number of Roman warships):
In the town a huge crowd assembled. Not only was the arrival of the pirates indicated by a raised fire from either a watch post or a hill, as it had always been done before, but the flames of the blazing ships themselves announced the disaster that had already happened and the danger to the remainder.

**20.** Caesar *The Gallic Wars* II, 33:
In the third watch the Gauls suddenly sallied out from the place in full strength . . . The alert was quickly sent by signal fires in accordance with Caesar's standing orders and the garrisons of the nearest forts rushed to the spot.

**21.** Caesar *The Civil Wars* III, 65 (Dyrrachium 48 BC):
Pompey was advancing on Marcellinus' camp, after killing many of our men and so causing considerable fear in the remaining cohorts . . . The information was relayed to Caesar from fort to fort by smoke, as was normal practice and he soon arrived in person with cohorts taken from some of the guard posts.

**22.** Onasander *The General* XXV, 3:
Once the first signaller shows his light, the second signals to the next, and so on in sequence, the third to the fourth and the fifth to the sixth, so that soon, over a range of many stades, the message sent by the first is known by everyone.

**23.** Frontinus *Strategemata* II, 5. 16. (translation by Dr B. Hoffmann) (Context not specified):
As it was known to be the custom that the Arabs used to signal the arrival of their enemies by smoke during the day and by fire at night, they ordered that these signals should continue without interruption but should cease upon the arrival of the enemy. The enemy

then thought, because of the lack of signals, that their arrival had gone undetected and so advanced too eagerly and were defeated.

**24.** Maurice *Strategikon* 7, 2.10:
If it has been impossible to collect forage . . . the servants should go out . . . escorted by patrols . . . They should be ordered to be on the alert for signals to warn them of any enemy approach, to be given from specific high and prominent positions, by smoke or trumpet call.

## Signals capable of more than one message

**25.** Thucydides *The Peloponnesian War* III, 80 (Corcyra 427 BC) (assuming the signal really carried all this information):
After ravaging the land until noon, the Peloponnesians sailed off again, but at around dusk, they were told by fire signal that a 60-strong squadron of Athenian ships was approaching from Leucas.

**26.** Xenophon *Hellenica* 6, 2, 33-4 (Corcyra 373 BC):
Iphicrates found out that 10 triremes were en route from Dionysius to reinforce the Spartans. He personally went to explore the ground to find a position from which any incoming ship could be spotted and from which signals could be seen in the city. He stationed men on lookout here and worked out with them what signals they were to give to say that the enemy were arriving and then to say when they were docked.

**27.** Polybius *Histories* X, 42. 7 (second Punic War. Operations in Greece):
To make sure that he would be aware of whatever was happening, he (Philip V of Macedon) sent orders to the Peparethians, and his generals in Phocis and Boeotia, that they were to inform him of events by fire signals sent directly to a mountain in Thessaly called Mt Tisaeus, which was well placed as it commanded an excellent a view of those areas.

**28.** Suetonius *The Twelve Caesars* Tiberius 65 (On Capri, a terrified Tiberius awaits the news of Sejanus's arrest. AD 31):
Tiberius even considered fleeing to some provincial army base and had a squadron of ships ready to evacuate him from the island, where he waited on a cliff for the distant fire signals to give news of whatever was to come.[2] He had ordered this in case his messengers were held up.

## The jamming of fire signals

**29.** Thucydides *The Peloponnesian War* III, 22 (Siege of Plataea, 427 BC):
Fire signals marking an enemy attack were transmitted to Thebes; but the Plataeans also lit a number of their own fire signals from their town wall, which they had prepared in

advance for the purpose. This was to make it impossible to understand the enemy's signals so as to prevent support arriving from Thebes, and to make sure that the Thebans would not have an accurate picture of the situation.

**30.** Polyaenus *Strategemata* 4, 19. 2 (translation provided by Dr J.P. Wild):
When the Plataeans were being besieged by the Spartans they broke through the surrounding siege wall at night. The Spartans gave the fire signal for 'Enemy' to Thebes to bring in extra troops, but the Plataeans then gave the fire signal for 'Friend' from their walls, whereupon the Thebans allowed themselves to be persuaded, by these signals, not to send help.

## The limitations of beacon signals

**31.** Polybius *Histories* X, 43. 1-10 (second century BC):
I don't think I can continue without a full discussion of fire signalling, which is now of the greatest military value, but which used to have major shortcomings. Timing is obviously important for success in any matter, but especially in war, and fire signals are the most efficient means of helping us. They can tell us what has only just happened or even what is currently happening and, with them, anyone who wishes can be kept informed even at a range of three, four, or more day's travel. Help can thus be summoned by signal surprisingly quickly when needed. At one time, fire signals were just beacons, and so were frequently of only limited use to their users. For they could only be used for prearranged signals and as real events are unpredictable, they could generally not be communicated by fire-signals. If we take the example I have just mentioned (in 27 above), one could send news that a fleet had arrived at Oreus, Peparethus or Chalcis, once one had arranged the relevant signals, but one could still not use fire signals to say that some of the inhabitants had changed sides, or been guilty of treachery, or that a massacre had happened in the town, or anything else of this nature. This sort of thing happens often but cannot be anticipated and it is generally the unexpected events which demand fast decisions and responses. Yet it was here that the earlier system broke down, because it is impossible to agree on a signal for what one cannot foresee.

## Daytime signals

**32.** Herodotus *The Histories* 6, 115 (Battle of Marathon 490 BC):
The Alcmaeonidae were accused of proposing this tactic [a flanking attack on the city] in Athens. It was claimed that they had a pact with the Persians and had signalled to them by raising a shield.

**33.** Aineias Tacticus 6.1-6.7 (fourth century BC) (translation by kind permission of Prof. D.J. Whitehead):
Daytime scouts too, must be posted in front of the city, at an elevated point visible from as great a distance as possible. At each point there should be at least three scouts chosen

... for their experience of war; this is to avoid any one scout's ignorantly supposing that something is important, signalling or reporting it to the city and causing needless trouble to the people there. In the absence of such places from which the signals are directly visible in the city there will have to be relay stations at various points to receive the signals as they are raised and transmit them to the city. Also, the daytime scouts must be fleet of foot, able, in circumstances where signalling is impossible and information has to be conveyed by word of mouth, to return quickly with the news even over the longest distances. But where the terrain is suitable for horses — and there are horses available — the best way of sending messages more quickly is by relays of horsemen. They should all have one and the same password (different from the one in the city): this is so that if they are captured by the enemy they will be in no position to reveal, either willingly or under duress, the password which the men in the city are using. Order the daytime scouts to raise their signals from time to time, just as the fire-signallers raise their torches.

**34.** Aineias Tacticus 7.1-7.4:
An enemy in the vicinity at harvest time will probably mean that much of the population will remain in the fields nearby fearful of their crops; so here is how they are to be gathered inside the city. First, at sunset, give a signal for those outside the walls to return to the city. If they are scattered across a wider area of land, use relay stations for the signal so as to bring everyone, or nearly everyone, into the town. After the signal for them to return give another for those in the city to prepare dinner, and a third for the guards to go to their posts. The way to do this, and to raise fire-signals, is described at greater length in my book *Preparations* [this does not survive]; to avoid treating the same topics twice I must leave them to be studied there.

**35.** Xenophon *Hellenica* 1, 1. 1-4 (Hellespont 411 BC):
Dorieus had sailed with 14 ships from Rhodes. He got in at dawn and was spotted by the Athenian watchman on duty that day, who signalled news of his arrival to the Athenian leaders.

**36.** Xenophon *Hellenica* II, 1. 27 (Aegospotami 405 BC):
As the Athenians sailed in, Lysander gave specific orders to those ships that had been detailed to shadow them. The moment they saw that the Athenians had landed and dispersed . . . they were to return halfway and signal with a shield.

**37.** Xenophon *Hellenica* V, 1. 27 (Percote 386 BC):
Antalcidas quickly overtook the slowest Athenian ships with his own fastest units, but told his leading squadron (presumably by signal) to stand on after those in front, rather than hitting the enemy's stragglers.

**38.** Diodorus Siculus 19. 17, 7:
Persia is split by many gullies and has numerous high, closely spaced watch posts where the natives with the loudest voices were posted. Since these stations were within earshot

of each other, messages could be passed from one to the next and so on until they reached the frontier of the (relevant) Satrapy.

**39.** Thucydides *The Peloponnesian War* I, 63 (Potidaea 432 BC):
As battle commenced, signals were made, and the men of Olynthus (which is about seven miles away and in sight of Potidaea) who were supposed to help the Potidaeans advanced a short distance with the intention of entering action . . . But the Athenians soon won and the signals were cancelled.

**40.** Thucydides *The Peloponnesian War* 8, 95 (Eretria 411 BC):
Agesandridas . . . sailed from Oropus, which is about seven miles by sea from Eretria. As he sailed to attack . . . a signal from Eretria to Oropus told the Peloponnesians when to put to sea.

**41.** Caesar *The Civil War* 1, 28 (Brundisium 49 BC):
The citizens of Brundisium were pro-Caesar as they were angered by maltreatment by Pompey's solders and Pompey's own insulting conduct. When they found out that he was planning to leave . . . they signalled the information from the roofs . . . The wall guards were withdrawn by prearranged signal and rushed down to the ships and Pompey sailed towards dusk.

**42.** Vegetius *De Rei Militaris* III, 5. 25:
When groups of men are separated from one another, they give each other signals by means of smoke in the daytime and fire by night.

## Recognition signals

**43.** Aineias Tacticus (fourth century BC) (translation by kind permission of Prof. D.J. Whitehead):
4.1: As a first priority signals should have been prearranged, so that men will not go unidentified as they approach.
4.5: In time of war when the enemy is nearby, the first requirement is that troops sent out from the city for any operation, on land or at sea, be furnished with both daytime and night-time signals for communicating with those still in the city. This is so that the latter can tell friend from foe, if enemies put in a sudden appearance.
4.6: And once the force has set out on its mission send some observers who will recognise the signals, so that those left behind can track its movements from as far out as possible; to be prepared for any eventuality in good time is most important.

## Carrier pigeons

**44.** Frontinus *Strategemata* III, 13.8 (translation provided by Dr B. Hoffmann) (Siege of Mutina 43 BC):

Hirtius tied letters with a hair to the necks of pigeons, which he had kept in the dark and starved. He then released them from a location as close to the city walls as he could get. Being eager for light and food, they headed for the highest of the buildings where they were caught by (Decimus) Brutus, who was thus informed about everything, especially after he had taught the pigeons to settle in those spots where he had put out food beforehand.

## Semaphore

**45.** Vegetius *De Rei Militaris* III, 5.30:
Many report what is happening by means of a beam mounted on the towers of a fort or city wall and which is sometimes raised and sometimes lowered.

**46.** Anon Byzant 261b, 5 (translation provided by Dr J.P. Wild):
These are the signals from which the signallers (*semeiophoroi*) get their name. The visible signals which, when moved in one way and then in the other have different meanings so that the generals can send instructions to their junior officers who can then pass them on to the soldiers.

## Signalling by torch combinations

**47.** Polybius *Histories* X, 45.6-47.4 (second century BC):
The latest technique was invented by Cleoxenus and Democleitus and refined by me. It is perfectly specific and can send any urgent message with precision. It does, however, require the greatest diligence and more exact attention in its handling. The procedure is this: one divides the alphabet into five parts each of five letters, apart from the last part which has one letter less, although this does not affect the process. Then both signal positions should acquire five tables and write one section of the letters on each. When one station wants to signal it should first raise two torches and wait until the receiver replies by doing the same. This tells both that the other is ready. Once these torches have been lowered, the transmitter first lifts the torches on the left-hand side in order to indicate which of the tablets is to be looked at: one torch for the first, two for the second and so on. Next, using the same principal, the right-hand torches are used to show which letter on this tablet the recipient should write down. Once they have agreed all this and each has gone to his station, they must obtain a double-barrelled *dioptra*. They need this equipment so that the receiver can see the torches on the right through the right-hand barrel, and the left-hand group with the left. Alongside this the tablets should be set up vertically and one must also set up a heavy screen in front of each of the right and left-hand groups the height of a man and 10ft wide[3] so that the signals can be made clearly visible by raising the torches above this screen and then hidden when lowered. Now that everyone on both sides is equipped and ready, if one wants to transmit, for example, that about one hundred of our soldiers have gone over to the enemy, he must first choose

words that express this with as few letters as possible. For example, here he might say 'Cretans a hundred deserted us'. In this version the number of letters is halved, but the meaning is the same. He writes this down on a tablet and then signals like this: the first letter is Kappa. This belongs to the second group of letters and is thus on the second tablet. He must, therefore, raise two torches on the left-hand side, so that the recipient knows that he needs to look at the second tablet. He then lifts up five torches on the right because Kappa is the fifth letter of the second section and the receiver can write this down on his tablet. Then he lifts up four torches on the left because Rho belongs to the fourth section and then puts up two on the right because it is the second letter of that section, whereupon the receiver writes down Rho and soon, by this method, he can transmit news of anything that happens with total certainty. Naturally one needs a large number of torches because one needs two signals for every letter transmitted. But if everything is properly prepared for the purpose, the operation presents no difficulties. Those at both ends must have practice before hand, however, so that in actual operations their transmissions will work perfectly.

**48.** Julius Africanus *Kestoi* 77 (third century AD) (translation provided by Dr J.P. Wild): The Romans have the following technique which seems to me to be amazing. If they want to communicate something by fire signal, they make the signals so: they select places that are suitable for making fire signals. They divide the fires into a right, a left and a middle fire so that they read alpha to theta from the left-hand one, iota to pi from the middle one and rho to omega from the right-hand fire. If they then signal 'alpha', they raise up the fire signal on the left once, for beta twice and for gamma three times. If they signal 'iota' they raise the middle fire once, for kappa twice and for lambda thrice, and if they want to signal rho, sigma or tau, they raise the right-hand signal once, twice or three times. In this way should you want to signal 'rho' you do not need to raise hundreds of fire signals, but only one with the right-hand torch. Those who receive the signals then de-code them in the same way, or pass them on to the next station.

## Signalling with water clocks

**49.** Philon *Mechanica* VII, 8.55-57 (third century BC) (translation provided by Dr J.P. Wild): One must produce a punctured copper or pottery vessel of no less than four measures capacity [*c.*150 litres].[4] Into this one puts a float with a rod inserted into it which is divided up into three finger breadth [*c.*5.55cm] graduations.[5] On each of these divisions is written one of the following messages: 'Ships'; 'Grain'; 'Wood'; 'Weapons'; 'Soldiers', or whatever else one may require for a siege, or any other purpose. Once this is written, then if fire signals are made at night to a given town, fort or watch post and the water is let out of the punctured vessel, then within the limits of the available signals, one can gather what the beleaguered require, so long as vessels are also available at these other sites, which are of exactly the same size, have identical punctures and have the same messages marked in the same places. This must be arranged in advance.

**50.** Polybius *Histories* X, 44.1-45.2 (second century BC):

Aineias . . . says [see 34 above] that [in order to overcome the limitations of simple beacon signals] people who want to send each other urgent messages by fire-signal need to get themselves two earthenware vessels of equal width and height, about three cubits tall and one cubit in diameter,[6] with corks slightly narrower than the mouths of the vessels. Through the middle of these corks they should attach a rod, divided into equal sections of three finger-widths, by clearly recognisable graduations and onto each of these divisions they should write one of the most important events in war. So, for example, on the first they might put 'Horsemen have invaded the country', on the second 'Heavy infantry', on the third 'Lightly armed troops', on the next 'Infantry and and cavalry' then 'Ships', 'Grain' and so forth until each field on the rod has some military event entered on it that it is anticipated might well occur under the prevailing circumstances. Once this is done, they should drill a hole of exactly the same size through both vessels so that water will drain from them at the same speed. Then they should fill them with water, float the corks and rods on the surface and then let the water run out through the holes at the same time. Naturally, since both sets of equipment are identical, the water will run out at the same rate and the two corks will sink together and more and more of the rods will become masked by the vessels. Once they have established by practical experiment that they do indeed work together at the same speed, they should take the vessels to the places where both will be making and looking out for fire signals. Now when one of the incidents marked on the rods actually happens one should raise a torch and wait until the observers on the receiving station reply. Once both torches are visible the transmitter should lower his torch and immediately let the water start to run out through the vessel's hole. As soon as the sinking float brings the section of the rod that carries the message he wants to send against the rim of the vessel, he should put up his torch again. The receivers must then immediately close their plug and look to see what message the rim of their vessel is indicating. This will be the same message that was transmitted providing that everything has been properly synchronised at both ends. This was certainly a small advance over signalling with prearranged signs, but even this method is still very uncertain. Because, obviously, is it not possible to anticipate everything that could happen, or if one could foresee it, to enter it all on the rod.

**51.** Polyaenus *Strategemata* VI, 16.2 (second century AD) (translation provided by Dr J.P. Wild):

When the Carthaginians were laying waste to Sicily they made two water clocks so that necessities could be sent from Africa as quickly as possible. The water clocks were exactly the same size and inscribed with identical circles and messages. The messages included such things as 'Ships are required', 'Freight vessels', 'Gold', 'Siege engines', 'Provisions', 'Cattle', 'Weapons', 'Infantry', 'Cavalry'.

After all these circles were inscribed they kept one of these water clocks in Sicily and sent the other to Carthage with the instructions that when they saw a raised signal fire they should watch out. If then a second fire was raised they should note at which circle this was done.[7] When they had read what was written there they should send whatever had been signalled for at once. In this manner the Carthaginians got everything ready for war as quickly as possible.

## Signalling by flare

**52.** Julius Africanus *Kestoi* 77 (third century AD) (translation provided by Dr J.P. Wild): Those who are concerned with fire signals should be chosen out of the mass and selected for their courage to ensure that they do not flee too soon out of fear of the enemy and abandon their showing of the fire signals. They must prepare brushwood, reeds, branches and hay in advance. This causes a great flame and thick smoke. One then uses the material to put on the fire and with this lets it flare up twice if one is not certain exactly what has happened, whether it concerns the movement of animals, fugitives or the enemy. If one recognises that it is to do with the enemy, who are advancing to fight, one lets the fire flare up three or four times and if there are a lot of them, even more than that. It is also possible, as has been described by some of the older writers, to express the enemy's number in thousands. One simply lets the fire flare up once for each 1000 men who seem to be involved. One must also be aware that the enemy often show themselves by day and then go back at night, they then keep quiet for several days before repeating the process. If the signals are lit on every appearance of the enemy, the people may initially flee, but eventually they will start to ignore the signals and stay in their houses so that when the enemy do come, they will take them by surprise. At the first appearance of the enemy, therefore, one must make the fire flare up just once or twice in distinct bursts and then stop. That will alert the people to be ready to flee without actually leaving their homes. If, however, many of the enemy appear, one repeats the signals, using fire at night and smoke during the daytime, so that the people will know what is meant. These signals must, however, be common to all and understood both by those who send them and by the recipients.

## Notes

1  This may suggest that this idea was a novelty. Certainly news of earlier defeats had been sent via the Persian Empire's efficient relay messenger service (Herodotus VIII 97-9).
2  It is possible that this system was limited to transmitting simply a) 'All is well', or b) 'run!', but it may have been far more sophisticated.
3  Assuming that Polybius, who was writing in Roman semi-captivity, is referring to the Roman foot of 296mm, this equals 2.96m (Dilke 1987, 26f).
4  The word used is *metretes*. The size of this unit varied according to area between 34.56l and 38.88l. The jars thus hold between 138.24l and 155.52l (Dilke 1987, 26).
5  *Daktyloi* = $\frac{1}{16}$ of a Greek foot. The foot varies with region but is commonly 296mm, so one finger-breadth = 18.5mm, making the graduations 5.55cm wide (Dilke 1987, 26).

6   Three different sizes of cubit were in general use, but the specific word used is *pechus* which is the standard cubit of *c*.44cm. The vessel is thus *c*.132cm high and *c*.44cm across. Assuming it to have been cylindrical, its capacity was, therefore, *c*.200.79l.

7   Polyaenus omits to say that the water should be allowed to flow out during the time between the two fire signals, but the sense is still reasonably clear.

# Appendix 2

## Location evidence for towers on *Limes* study sector 2

9/120.  **Probable**, but position is vague.
9/121.  **KNOWN** from aerial photography.
9/122.  **KNOWN**, but position is vague.
9/123.  **Assumed**.
9/124.  **KNOWN**.
9/125.  **Assumed**.
9/126.  **KNOWN**.
9/127.  **KNOWN**.
9/128.  **KNOWN**. *Kleinkastell*.
9/129.  Surface feature once visible.
9/130.  **Assumed**.
9/131.  **Assumed**.
9/132.  Small finds ploughed up.
9/133.  **Assumed**.
9/134.  **KNOWN**.
9/135.  **Assumed**.
9/136.  **KNOWN**.
9/137.  **Assumed**.
12/1.   **KNOWN**.
12/2.   **KNOWN**.
12/3.   **KNOWN**.
12/4.   **Assumed**.
12/5.   **Assumed**.
12/6.   **Assumed**.
12/7.   **KNOWN**.
12/8.   **KNOWN**.
12/9.   **KNOWN**.
12/10.  **Assumed**.
12/11.  **KNOWN**.
12/12.  **KNOWN**.
12/13.  **KNOWN**.
12/14.  **KNOWN**.
12/15.  **Assumed**.

12/16.   **Probable**. Once visible as a mound.

12/17.   **KNOWN**.

12/18.   **Assumed**, but excellent position.

12/19.   **Probable**. Claimed excavation 1888.

12/20.   **Assumed**.

12/21.   **KNOWN**.

12/22.   **KNOWN**. *Kleinkastell*.

12/23.   **KNOWN**.

12/24.   **KNOWN**.

12/25.   **KNOWN**.

12/26.   **Assumed**.

12/27.   **Assumed**.

12/28.   **Assumed**.

12/29.   **Assumed**.

12/30.   **Assumed**.

12/31.   **Assumed**.

12/32.   **Assumed**.

12/33.   **KNOWN**. *Kleinkastell*.

12/34.   Stones and charcoal found.

12/35.   Possible remains under chapel.

12/36.   **Assumed** on bend in the line.

12/37.   **KNOWN**.

12/38.   **Assumed**.

12/39.   **Assumed**.

12/40.   **Assumed**.

12/41.   Stones and mortar found.

12/42.   **KNOWN**.

12/43.   **Assumed**.

12/44.   **Assumed**.

12/45.   **KNOWN**.

12/46.   **KNOWN**.

12/47.   **?KNOWN**.

12/48.   **Assumed**.

12/49.   Stones and mortar found.

12/50.   Rubble mound.

12/51.   Stones and slates found.

12/52.   **Assumed**.

12/53.   **Assumed**.

12/54.   **Probable**. Some excavation and finds evidence.

12/55.   **Assumed**.

12/56.   Stones, mortar and slates found.

12/57.   **Assumed**.

12/58.   **Assumed**.

12/59.   **KNOWN**.

12/60.   **KNOWN**.
12/61.   Stones found.
12/62.   **Assumed**.
12/63.   **Assumed**.
12/64.   **Assumed**.
12/65.   **Assumed**.
12/66.   **KNOWN**.
12/67.   **KNOWN**.
12/68.   **KNOWN**.
12/69.   **Assumed**.
12/70.   **Assumed**.
12/71.   **Assumed**.
12/72.   **Assumed**.
12/73.   **Assumed**.
12/74.   **KNOWN**.
12/75.   **KNOWN**.
12/76.   **Assumed**.
12/77.   **KNOWN**.
12/78.   **Assumed**.
12/79.   **Assumed**.
12/80.   **Assumed**.
12/81.   **KNOWN**. Dalkingen.
12/82.   **Assumed**.
12/83.   **KNOWN**.
12/84.   **KNOWN**.
12/85.   **KNOWN**.
12/86.   Rubble found.
12/87.   Stones found.
12/88.   Folklore.
12/89.   Folklore and surface mound.
12/90.   **Assumed**.
12/91.   **Assumed**.
12/92.   **Assumed**.
12/93.   **Assumed**.
12/94.   **Assumed**.
12/95.   **Assumed**.
12/96.   **KNOWN**, but position vague.
12/97.   **Assumed**.
12/98.   Building found 400m behind line.
12/99.   **Assumed**.
12/100.  **Assumed**.
12/101.  **Probable**.
12/102.  **Assumed**.
12/103.  **KNOWN**.

12/104.  **Assumed**.
12/105.  **Assumed**.
12/106.  **Assumed**.
12/107.  **KNOWN**.

# Bibliography

*Abbreviations*

ORL: Fabricius, E., Hettner, F. & von Sarway, O. 1894-1937 *Der obergermanisch-raetische Limes des Römerreiches*, Berlin and Leipzig.

RIB:  Collingwood, R.G. & Wright, R.P. 1965 *The Roman Inscriptions of Britain*, Oxford.


## Ancient sources

Aeschylus *The Agamemnon*

Africanus *The Kestoi*

Aineias Tacticus *On the Defence of Fortified Positions*

Ammianus Marcellinus *The History*

Anon *The Scriptores Historiae Augustae*

Appian *The Spanish Wars*

Appian *The Civil Wars*

Aristophanes *Lysistrata*

Aristotle *De Mundo*

Caesar *The Gallic Wars*

Caesar *The Civil War*

Cicero *The Verrine Orations*

Diodorus Siculus *World History*

Frontinus *The Strategemata*

Herodotus *The Histories*

Heron of Alexandria *Rationes Dimetiendi et Commentatio Dioptrica*

Homer *The Iliad*

Maurice *The Strategikon*

Onasander *The General*

Pausanias *The Guide to Greece*

Philon *The Mechanica*

Polyaenus *The Strategemata*

Plutarch *The Parallel Lives*

Polybius *The Histories*

Suetonius *The Twelve Caesars*

Tacitus *The Germania*

Thucydides *The Peloponnesian War*

Vegetius *De Rei Militaris*

Vitruvius *De architectura*

Xenophon *The Hellenica*

## Modern writers

Anon, Undated *Lußbildarchäologie in Hessen*, Wiesbaden.

Baatz, D. 1971 'Zum Archäologischen Nachweis eines Alamanneneinfalles am obergermanischen Limes unter Elagabal', *Bonner Jahrbuch*, 171, 377ff.

Baatz, D. 1980 'Die gestempelten Ziegel aus den Kleinkastellen Haselheck bei Echzell und Maisel bei Glashütten', *Fundberichte aus Hessen*, 19/20, 679ff.

Baatz, D. & Herrmann, F.R. (ed.) 1989 *Die Römer in Hessen* (2nd ed.), Stuttgart.

Bellhouse, R.L. 1955 'The Roman Fort at Burrow Walls Near Workington', *CW* (2), 55, 30-45.

Bellhouse, R.L. 1962 'Moricambe in Roman Times and Sites on the Cumberland Coast', *CW* (2), 62, 56-72.

Bellhouse, R.L. 1969 'Roman Sites on the Cumberland Coast 1966-67', *CW* (2), 69, 79-101.

Bellhouse, R.L. 1970 'Roman Sites on the Cumberland Coast 1968-1969', *CW* (2), 70, 9-47

Bellhouse, R.L. 1981 'Roman Sites on the Cumberland Coast : Milefortlet 20, Low Mire', *CW* (2), 81, 7-14.

Bellhouse, R.L. 1981 'Hadrian's Wall: The Limiting Ditches in the Cardurnock Peninsular', *Britannia*, 12, 135-42.

Bellhouse, R.L. 1989 *Roman Sites on the Cumberland Coast, A New Schedule of Coastal Sites*, Kendal.

Bellhouse, R.L. & Richardson, G.G.S. 1982 'The Trajanic Fort at Kirkbride; The Terminus Of The Stanegate Frontier', *CW* (2), 82, 35-50.

Binns, M. 1971 'Four Laws, 77, NY 905830' *Arch. Ael.* (4), 49, 131-4.

Birley, E.B. 1961 *Research on Hadrian's Wall*, Kendal.

Bowman, A.K. & Thomas, J.D. 1991 'A Military Strength Report From Vindolanda', *J.R.S.*, 81, 62-73.

Braasch, O. 1983 *Luftbildarchäologie in Süddeutschland*, Stuttgart.

Breeze, D.J. 1972 'Excavations at the Roman Fort of Carrawburgh, 1967-1969', *Arch. Ael.* (4), 50, 87.

Breeze, D.J. & Dobson, B. 2000 *Hadrian's Wall*, 4th ed., London.

Calder, W.M. 1922 'The Geography of the Beacon Passage in the Agamemnon', *Classical Review* (Old Series), 36, 155.

Caprino, C. 1955 *La Colonna Di Marco Aurelio*, Rome.

Casey, P.J. & Savage, M. 1980 'Coins From the Excavations at High Rochester in 1852 and 1855', *Arch. Ael.* (5), 8, 75-88.

Cichorius, C. 1900 *Die Reliefs der Traianssäule*, Berlin.

Collingwood, R.G. 1915 'Roman Remains From Maiden Castle on Stainmore', *CW* (2), 15, 192-3.

Collingwood, R.G. 1927 'Maiden Castle in Stainmore', *CW* (2), 27, 170-7.

Collingwood, R.G. 1930 'Hadrian's Wall a System of Numerical References', *P.S.A.N.* (4), 4, 179- 87.

Collingwood, R.G. 1931 'A Roman Fortlet on Barrock Fell Near Low Hasket', *CW* (2), 31, 111-18.

Collingwood, R.G. & Wright, R.P. 1965 *The Roman Inscriptions of Britain*, Oxford.

Crow, J.G. 1987 'Peel Gap', *Current Archaeology*, 108 (Nov), 14.

Crow, J.G. 1991 'A Review of Current Research on the Turrets and Curtain of Hadrian's Wall', *Britannia*, 22, 51-63.

Czysz, W. 1977 'Archäologische Nachuntersuchung am Kleinkastell Neuwirtshaus bei Hanau.', *Neues Magazin für Hanauische Geschichte*, 6, Nr 5, 121ff.

Denniston, J.D. & Page, D. (eds) 1957 *Aeschylus: Agamemnon*, Oxford.

Diels, H. 1914 *Antike Technik*, Leipzig and Berlin.

Dilke, O.A.W. 1971 *The Roman Land Surveyors*, Newton Abbot.

Dilke, O.A.W. 1987 *Mathematics and Measurement*, London.

Dobson, B. 1986, 'The Function of Hadrian's Wall', *Arch. Ael.* (5), 14, 1-30.

Donaldson, G.H. 1985 'Roman Military Signalling on the North British frontiers', *Arch. Ael.* (5), 13, 19-24.

Donaldson, G.H. 1988 'Signalling Communications and the Roman Imperial Army', *Britannia*, 19, 349-56.

Esmond Cleary, A.S. 1985 'Roman Britain 1994, England', *Britannia*, 26, 342-70.

Fabricius E., Hettner, F. & von Sarway, O. 1894-1937 *Der obergermanisch-raetische Limes des Römerreiches*, Berlin and Leipzig.

Farrar, R.A.H. 1980 'Roman Signal Stations Over the Stainmore and Beyond', in Hanson, W.S. & Keppie, L.J.F. (eds) *Roman Frontier Studies 1979*, B.A.R. 71I, 211-32.

Ferguson, R.S. 1897 'Sites of Local Beacons: Cumberland and Westmorland' *CW* (1), 14, 140.

Firbas, F. 1930 'Eine Flora aus dem Brunnenschlamm des Römerkastells Zugmantel' *Saalburg Jahrbuch*, 7, 75ff.

Fox, A. 1967 'Martinhoe and Old Burrow', in *Studien zu den Militärgrenzen Roms* Proceedings of the 6th International Limes Congress, Köln, 15-20.

Fraenkel, E. 1950 *Aeschylus: Agamemnon*, Vol. 2 (Commentary), Oxford.

Frere, S.S. 1986 'Roman Britain in 1985', *Britannia*, 17, 363-454.

Frere, S.S. 1987 *Britannia* (3rd ed.), London.

Glendinning, B. & Dunwell, A. 2000, 'Excavations of the Gask Frontier Tower and Temporary Camp at Blackhill Wood, Ardoch, Perth & Kinross', *Britannia*, 31, 255-90.

Gudea, N. 1997 'Die Verteidigung der Provinz Dacia Porolissensis Zwischen Mauersperre und Verteidigung in der Tiefe', in Groenman van Waaterings, W. *et al.* (ed.), *Roman Frontier Studies 1995*, Proceedings of the 16th International Congress of Roman Frontier Studies, Oxford, 13-24.

Haigh, D. & Savage, M. 1984 'Sewingshields', *Arch. Ael.* (5), 12, 33-148.

Hanson, W.S. & Maxwell, G.S. 1983, 'Minor Enclosures on the Antonine Wall at Wilderness Plantation', *Britannia*, 14, 227-44.

Hartley, B.R. & Fitts, R.L. 1988 *The Brigantes*, Gloucester.

Helmke, P. 1910 *Römische specula über einer Germanischen Anlage auf dem Johannisberg bei Bad Nauhei*, Bad Nauheim.

Herrmann, F.R. 1985 *Der Glauberg am Ostrand der Wetterau, Archäologische Denkmäler in Hessen*, 51, Wiesbaden.

Herrmann, F.R. 1986 *Der Dünsberg bei Gießen*, Archäologische Denkmäler in Hessen, 60, Wiesbaden.

Higham, N.J. & Jones, G.D.B., 1985 *The Carvetii*, Gloucester.

Hodgson, N. 1997 'Relationships between Roman River Frontiers and Artificial Frontiers', in Groenman-van Waateringe, W *et al.* (ed.), *Roman Frontier Studies 1995*, Proceedings of the XVIth International Congress of Roman Frontier Studies, Oxford, 61-6.

Hodgson, N. 2000 'The Stanegate: a frontier rehabilitated', *Britannia*, 31, 11-22.

Hoernle, E.S. 1921 *The Problem of the Agamemnon*, Oxford.

Holder, P.A. 1980 *Studies in the Auxilia of the Roman Army from Augustus to Trajan*, BAR International series 70.

Holder, P.A. 1982 *The Roman Army in Britain*, London.

Jarrett, M.G. 1976 *Maryport, Cumbria: A Roman Fort and its Garrison* (C&W Extra Series 22), Kendal.

Jones, G.D.B. 1976 'The Western Extension of Hadrian's Wall: Bowness to Cardurnock', *Britannia*, 7, 236-43.

Jones, G.D.B. 1978 'Concept and Development in Roman Frontiers', *Bull J. Rylands Library*, 61, 115-44.

Jones, G.D.B. 1982 'The Solway Frontier: Interim Report 1976-81', *Britannia*, 13, 283-98.

Jones, G.D.B. 1991 'The Emergence of the Tyne Solway Frontier' in Maxfield, V.A. & Dobson, M.J. (ed.) *Roman Frontier Studies 1989*, Proceedings of the XVth International Congress of Roman Frontier Studies, Exeter, 98-107.

Jones, G.D.B. 1993 'Excavations on a Coastal Tower, Hadrian's Wall: Campfield Tower 2B, Bowness-on-Solway', *Manchester Archaeological Bull*, 8, 31-9.

Jorns, W.W. 1967 'Das Kleinkastell Degerfeld bei Butzbach, Kr, Friedberg (Hessen)' *Saalburg Jahrbuch*, 24, 12ff.

Keen, A.G. forthcoming 'The Beacons Speech (Aeschylus Agamemnon 281-311)'.

Keppie, L.J.F. & Breeze, D.J. 1981 'Some Excavations on the Line of the Antonine Wall 1957-80', *Proc. Soc. Antiq. Scot.*, 111, 229-47.

Keppie, L.J.F. & Walker, J.J. 1981 'Tollpark', in Keppie, L.J.F. & Breeze, D.J. 'Some Excavations on the Line of the Antonine Wall 1957-80', *Proc. Soc. Antiq. Scot.*, 111, 229-47.

Kitchen, F. 1988 *Fire Over England, The Armada Beacons*, Brighton.

Knapp, R. 1973 'Die Vegetation der Umgebung von Butzbach in der Gegenwart und zur Römerzeit', *Saalburg Jahrbuch*, 30, 113ff.

Knörzer, K.H. 1973 'Römerzeitliche Pflanzenreste aus einem Brunnen in Butzbach, Hessen', *Saalburg Jahrbuch*, 33, 71ff.

Kofler, F. 1898 'Straßenturm im Wolfersheimer Walde', *Westdeutsche Zeitschrift*, 17, Limesblatt, 767ff.

Körtüm, K. 1998 'Zur Datierung der römischen Militäranlagen im obergermanisch-rätischen *Limes* gebiet, Chronologische Untersuchungen anhand der Münzfunde', *Saalburg Jahrbuch*, 49, 5-65.

Kröll, W. & Schönberger, H. 1965 'Untersuchungen am Limes bei Kastell Arnsburg', *Saalburg Jahrbuch*, 22, 12ff.

Leiner, W. 1982 *Der Signaltechnik Der Antike*, Stuttgart.

Lepper, F. & Frere, S.S. 1988 *Trajan's Column*, Gloucester.

Luttwak, E.N. 1976 *The Grand Strategy of the Roman Empire*, Baltimore.

Mackensen, M. 1989 'Frühkaiserzeitliche Kleinkastelle an der oberen Donau', *Zivile und Militarische Structuren im Nordwesten der römischen Provinz Raetien*, 3rd Heidenheimer Archäologie Colloquium, Heidenheim, 13ff.

Mann, J.C. 1974 'The Frontiers of the Principate', *ANRW*, II, principat 1, Berlin, 508-33.

McCord, N. & Jobey, G. 1971 'Notes on Air Reconnaissance in Northumberland and Durham II', *Arch. Ael.* (4), 49, 119-30.

Merriam, A.C. 1890 'Telegraphing Among the Ancients', *Papers of the Archaeological Institute of America*, Classical series 3, 1.

Mildenberger, G. 1978 'Die germanische Besiedlung des Dünsberges', *Fundberichte aus Hessen*, 17/18, 157ff.

Parker, S.T. 1986 *Romans and Saracens: A History of the Arabian Frontier*, Winona Lake.

Poidebard, A. 1934 *La Trace de Rome Dans le Désert de Syrie*, Paris.

Potter, T.W. 1979 *Romans in NW England* (C&W Research series 1), Kendal.

Poulter, J. 1998 'The Date of the Stanegate and a Hypothesis About the Manner and Timing of the Construction of Roman Roads in Britain', *Arch. Ael.* (5), 26, 49-58.

Richardson, G.G.S. 1977 'A Romano-British Farmstead at Fingland, Cumberland', *CW* (2), 77, 53-60.

Richmond, I.A. 1933 'The Tower at Gillalees Beacon', *CW* (2), 33, 241-5.

Richmond, I.A. 1936 'Excavations at High Rochester and Risingham', *Arch. Ael.* (4), 13, 170-98.

Richmond, I.A. 1940 'The Romans in Redesdale', in Northumberland County History Committee, *A History of Northumberland*, Newcastle upon Tyne, 63-154.

Richmond, I.A. 1951 'A Roman Arterial Signalling System in the Stainmore Pass', in Grimes, W.F. (ed.) *Aspects of Archaeology*, London, 293-302.

Richmond, I.A. & Hodgson, K.S. 1934 'Excavations at Castlesteads', *CW* (2), 34, 159-65.

Rivet, A.L.F. & Smith, C. 1979 *The Place Names of Roman Britain*, London.

Robinson, P. 1990 'The A66 Archaeology Project', *Current Archaeology*, 122 (Nov), 62-7.

Rösch, R. 1984 'Botanische Funde aus römischen Brunnen in Murrhardt Rems-Murr-Kreis', *AABW*, 114ff.

St Joseph, J.K. 1951 'Air Reconnaissance in North Britain', *J.R.S.*, 41, 52-65.

Schönberger, H. 1957 'Das Kastell Altenstadt zum äußeren obergermanischen Limes', *Germania*, 35, 83ff.

Schönberger, H. 1969 'The Roman Frontier in Germany: An Archaeological Survey.', *J.R.S.*, 59, 144-97.

Schönberger, H. 1979 'Die Namensstempel auf glatter Sigillata aus dem Erdkastell der Saalburg, Mit einem Beitrag von B.Hartley', *Saalburg Jahrbuch*, 27, 21ff.

Schönberger, H. 1985 'Die römischen Truppenlager der frühen und mittleren Kaiserzeit zwischen Nordsee und Inn', *Bericht der Römisch-Germanischen Kommission*, 66, 321.

Schönberger, H. & Simon, H.G. 1983 'Die Kastelle in Altenstadt', *Limesforschungen*, 22.

Seitz, G. 1989 'Pohlheim-Holzheim, römisches Limeskastell', *Denkmalpflege in Hessen*, 11ff.

Selkirk, R. 1983 *The Piercebridge Formula*, Cambridge.

Selkirk, R. 1987 'Roman Signal Stations', *Archaeology Today*, Vol. 8, No 1 (Feb), 126-31.

Simon, A. 1969 *The Search for Planet X*, New York.

Simon, H.G. 1968 'Das Kleinkastell Degerfeld bei Butzbach', *Saalburg Jahrbuch*, 25, 5ff.

Simpson, F.G. 1930 'The Roman Fort at Newbrough', *P.S.A.N.* (4), 4, 163-5.

Simpson, F.G. 1934 'Boothby, Castle Hill', *CW* (2), 34, 154-5.

Simpson, F.G. & McIntyre, J. 1933 'Pike Hill', *CW* (2), 33, 271-4.

Simpson, F.G., Richmond, I.A., Hodgson, K.S. & St Joseph, J.K. 1936 'The Stanegate', *CW* (2), 36, 182-91.

Southern, P. 1990 'Signalling Versus Illumination on Roman Frontiers', *Britannia*, 21, 233-42.

Steer, K.A. 1957 'The Nature and Purpose of the Expansions on the Antonine Wall', *Proc. Soc. Antiq. Scot.*, 90, 161-9.

Streckham, H.U. 1968 'Vegetationsgeschichtliche Untersuchung einer Römer-zeitlichen Torfbildung bei Butzbach in Hessen', *Saalburg Jahrbuch*, 17, 61ff.

Topping, P. 1987 'A New Signal Station in Cumbria', *Britannia*, 13, 298-9.

Verrall, A. 1904 *The Agamemnon of Aeschylus*, London.

Wagner, P. 1986 'Zum Kastellvicus des Kastells Oberflorstadt', *Proceedings of the 13th International Limes Congress*, Stuttgart, 281ff.

White, G.L. 1989 'Überlegungen zur Donaulimesdarstelung auf der Traianssäule in Rom', *Germania*, 67, 179-87.

Woodfield, C. 1965 'Six Turrets on Hadrian's Wall', *Arch. Ael.* (4), 43, 87-200.

Woodfield, P. 1966 'Barcombe Hill, Thorngrafton', *Arch. Ael.* (4), 44, 71-8.

Woolliscroft, D.J. 1988 'The Outpost System of Hadrian's Wall, An Outer *Limes*?', *British Archaeology*, 6 (March/April), 22-5.

Woolliscroft, D.J. 1989 (a) 'Signalling and the Design of Hadrian's Wall', *Arch. Ael.* (5), 17, 5-20.

Woolliscroft, D.J. 1989 (b) 'Elevated Archaeological Photography', *British Archaeology*, 13, 18-21.

Woolliscroft, D.J. 1990 'Barron's Pike, Possible Roman Signal Tower', *CW* (2), 90, 280-1.

Woolliscroft, D.J. 1993 'Signalling and the Design of the Gask Ridge System', *Proc. Soc. Antiq. Scot.*, 123, 291-314.

Woolliscroft, D.J. 1996 'Signalling and the Design of the Antonine Wall', *Britannia*, 27, 153-78.

Woolliscroft, D.J. forthcoming (a) 'Roman sites on the Antonine Wall at Garnhall, Cumbernauld', *Proc. Soc. Antiq. Scot.*

Woolliscroft, D.J. forthcoming (b) *The Roman Frontier on the Gask Ridge, Perth & Kinross*, TAFAC Monograph 3.

Woolliscroft, D.J. & Hoffmann, B. 1997 'The Roman Gask System Tower at Greenloaning, Perth & Kinross', *Proc. Soc. Antiq. Scot.*, 127, 563-76.

Woolliscroft, D.J. & Hoffmann, B. 1998 'The Roman Gask Series Tower at Shielhill South, Perth & Kinross. Excavations in 1973 and 1996', *Proc. Soc. Antiq. Scot.*, 128, 441-60.

Woolliscroft, D.J. & Jones, G.D.B. forthcoming *Excavations at Silloth and Fingland Rigg on the Cumbrian Coast*.

Woolliscroft, D.J., Nevell, M.D. & Swain, S.A.M. 1989 'The Roman Site on Grey Hill, Bewcastle, Cumbria', *CW* (2), 89, 69-76.

Woolliscroft, D.J. & Swain, S.A.M. 1991 'The Roman "Signal" Tower at Johnson's Plain, Cumbria', *CW* (2), 91, 19-30.

Woolliscroft, D.J., Swain, S.A.M. & Lockett, N.J. 1992 'Barcombe B, A Second Roman "Signal Tower" on Barcombe Hill', *Arch. Ael.* (5), 20, 57-62.

# Index